FORGED IN THE FIRE

A leadership fable of Resilience and Triumph

How to overcome the mid career
crisis and accelerate your career ?

SURA MUKKAVILLI

FORGED IN THE FIRE

A leadership fable of Resilience and Triumph

SURA MUKKAVILLI

Bonus

"The beautiful thing about learning is that nobody can take it away from you." – B.B. King

Please register on https://clap.skillculture.in . You will receive a coupon code / courses worth Rs. 20,000 free of cost.

Please go to https://www.futureproofleader.in/fitf for various resources, downloads, assessments and more.

Copyright

Copyright © 2024 by Sura Mukkavilli

All rights reserved.

Dedication

To my dad.

Table of Contents

Acknowledgments

At the outset, I would like to thank my wife, Annapurna, for standing by me throughout my career and helping me to become what I am today.

I would also like to thank my tiny twins Vishnu and Karthika for allowing me to steal the time I am supposed to give them.

I am grateful to my parents and brother for their constant support and encouragement throughout my journey.

I would not have been able to complete my book without their support and encouragement.

Introduction

Navigating the New World of Work

We live in an age of rapid change, where the rules of the game are constantly evolving. Every day, we hear about the latest technological breakthroughs, from AI and machine learning to automation and big data.

These innovations promise to revolutionize how we work, offering unprecedented gains in efficiency and productivity. Yet, despite these advances, many of us grapple with a growing sense of uncertainty.

Why? Because while technology is transforming the workplace, it's also creating new challenges—challenges that can't be solved by software or algorithms alone.

As professionals, we're expected to do more with less, to adapt quickly, and to stay ahead of the curve in an increasingly competitive environment.

But beyond the demands for technical proficiency, we face even greater pressures: to connect with others, to lead with empathy, to make sound decisions under pressure, and to persevere in the face of setbacks.

In today's fast-paced and ever-changing corporate world, the ability to navigate challenges with resilience, adaptability, and strategic thinking is no longer a luxury—it's a necessity.

Leaders are constantly tested by unforeseen obstacles, tight deadlines, and high-stakes decisions that can make or break their careers.

In such an environment, great leaders are distinguished by their ability to stay calm under pressure, think critically, and lead purposefully.

"Forged in the Fire tells the story of Ram and Priya, two corporate leaders who faced some of the most intense challenges of their careers.

Through grit, growth, and unwavering determination, they not only overcame these challenges but transformed them into opportunities for success.

This book is not just a narrative; it's a guide to understanding the key traits and strategies that every leader needs to thrive in difficult circumstances.

Who will benefit from this book?

This book is designed for:

- Aspiring Leaders: Individuals looking to step into leadership roles and seeking practical insights on how to prepare for the challenges ahead.

- Current Leaders and Managers: Those who are already in leadership positions and want to refine their approach, improve their resilience, and learn new strategies for handling high-pressure situations.

- Entrepreneurs: Business owners who need to navigate the complexities of running a company while maintaining a strong leadership presence.

- Students of Business and Management: Individuals studying leadership, management, or organizational behavior, who want to see real-world applications of the theories they are learning.

If you are not sure, ask yourself the following questions:

- Are you trying to balance the allure of new technologies with the need for deep, thoughtful leadership?

- Do you find yourself navigating complex relationships at work, where Emotional Intelligence is just as important as technical skill?

- Are you under pressure to deliver results, even when the path forward isn't clear?

- Do you sometimes feel overwhelmed by the pace of change, struggling to stay resilient in the face of uncertainty?

If any of these questions resonate, this book is for you.

The reality is that while AI and other tools can enhance our productivity, they can't replace the core human skills that are crucial for success. These skills help us connect with others, think critically, lead effectively, and bounce back from adversity. In a world where technological prowess is increasingly taken for granted, these human skills will set you apart.

Who will NOT benefit from this book?

While this book offers valuable lessons for a wide range of readers, it may not be as beneficial for:

- Individuals Looking for Quick Fixes: This book emphasizes the importance of long-term growth, resilience, and strategic thinking. This might not be the right resource if you're looking for easy shortcuts or quick wins.

- Readers Uninterested in Leadership Development: If you're not interested in developing your leadership skills or learning about the challenges of corporate leadership, this book may not align with your needs.

Methodology and What the Reader Can Expect

This book takes a narrative approach, using the story of Ram and Priya to illustrate key leadership principles in action. The methodology is straightforward: Through engaging storytelling, the book demonstrates how real-world challenges can be addressed with practical strategies and a resilient mindset.

Readers can expect to:

- Learn Key Leadership Frameworks: The book introduces and demonstrates several practical frameworks for effective communication, showing how they can be applied to real-life scenarios.

- Gain Insights into Problem-Solving and Decision-Making: Ram and Priya's challenges show readers how critical thinking, adaptability, and strategic planning are essential for overcoming obstacles.

Reflect on Personal Growth and Resilience: The book encourages readers to consider their leadership journey, offering insights into how to build resilience, lead with integrity, and maintain balance in the face of pressure.

Conclusion

Forged in the Fire is more than just a story—it's a roadmap for leaders at all stages of their careers. Whether you're just starting out or looking to enhance your leadership capabilities, this book offers valuable lessons and inspiration to help you navigate the complexities of modern leadership.

The journey of Ram and Priya serves as a powerful reminder that with the right mindset, tools, and support, any challenge can be transformed into an opportunity for growth and success.

This isn't just another book about leadership theory or management tactics. It's a practical guide designed to help you thrive in the real world—where the stakes are high, the pressure is on, and the need for human-centered leadership has never been greater.

As you read through the pages of this book, you'll see how Priya and Ram navigate the complexities of their roles, learning valuable lessons that you can apply to your own career. You'll find yourself relating to their struggles, celebrating their victories, and most importantly, gaining the tools you need to succeed in your own professional journey.

I invite you to embark on this journey with us—to explore, to reflect, and to grow. The world of work is changing, but with the right mindset, skills, and strategies, you can not only navigate these changes—you can lead them.

Through the journey of Priya and Ram, you'll discover practical frameworks and insights that address the very challenges you face in your daily work. You'll learn how to:

- Lead with Emotional Intelligence to build stronger relationships and navigate difficult conversations.
- Apply Critical Thinking to make informed decisions, even in complex or ambiguous situations.
- Stay Resilient in the face of setbacks, using adversity as a springboard for growth.
- Communicate Persuasively to inspire and influence those around you.
- Resolve Conflicts and build consensus in a way that strengthens teams and drives results.

Welcome to the new world of work. Let's dive in.

SuRaM

Section 1

The Struggle and the Awakening

Chapter 1

Cracks in the Armor

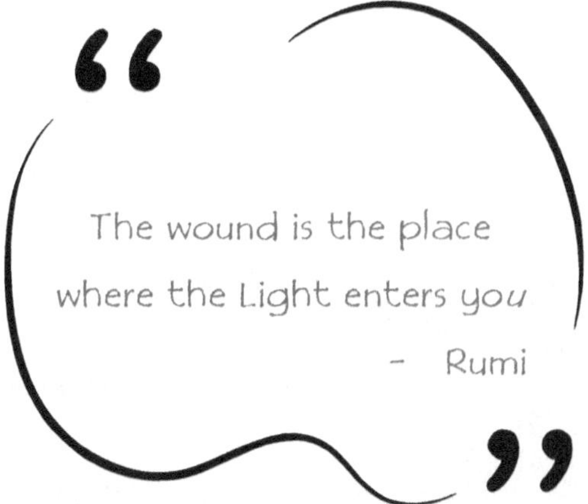

It was 9 PM on a chilly evening when Priya's phone buzzed with an urgent message from Sharma, the CEO of ClickFlix. The office was almost empty, the only sound being the hum of the air conditioning and the occasional clatter of a keyboard from his secretary.

Priya, who had just returned home after a long day, sighed as she read the message: 'Need you to prepare the final report for Atul's project tomorrow. I know our scheduled delivery is 10 days away, but the client insists on closing it faster. Use the AI tools you've just learned. Ram will be working on this as well. Expect a draft by 6 AM.'

Priya knew this was no ordinary task. Atul was ClickFlix's most valuable client, and this presentation could secure a multi-million dollar contract, a deal that could significantly boost the company's growth.

They had been working on this project for 30 days, and the presentation deadline was clearly two weeks away. The pressure was immense, but Priya felt a surge of confidence.

After all, she and Ram had just completed a rigorous digital transformation workshop, earning certifications in Gen AI and prompt engineering. Armed with these new skills, she felt ready to take on the challenge.

On the other side of the city, Ram received the same message. His reaction was a mix of excitement and anxiety. The project's importance was evident, and while he trusted his newly acquired AI skills, he couldn't shake off a feeling of unease. The tools were powerful, but were they enough to meet Sharma's exacting standards?

By midnight, both Priya and Ram were deep into their work. They used various AI tools to analyze data, generate insights, and draft the initial report. The process was fast—almost too fast. Within hours, they had a document that seemed comprehensive and polished, a report that they hoped would exceed Atul's expectations. They exchanged messages, feeling accomplished as the report took shape. At 7:30 AM, Priya and Ram sent their drafts to Sharma, confident they had nailed the task. But just an hour later, Sharma called a meeting.

Sharma sat behind his large desk, eyes scanning the project report that Priya and Ram had hastily prepared. His brow furrowed deeper with each page he turned. The room was tense as Priya and Ram stood before him, their anxiety evident.

Sharma finally looked up, his voice cutting through the silence like a knife.

His tone was unusually stern. 'There are gaps in this report,' he said, flipping through the pages on his tablet. 'Critical aspects are missing. This isn't just about data; it's about telling a story and providing insights that Atul can use. You've let the AI do the thinking for you, but it's shallow. You need to fix this fast. The presentation is in a few hours.'

The words hit Priya and Ram like a ton of bricks. They had relied too heavily on AI, assuming it would cover all bases. They needed to delve deeper and have thought critically about the insights they were presenting. The reality was sinking in—they had much more work and very little time to do it. The risk of disappointing Atul and losing the contract was a heavy burden.

Ram, feeling the weight of the criticism, took a step forward. "Mr. Sharma, we understand the urgency, but to make the necessary corrections—especially with the depth and detail required—we need more time. If we rush it again, we might miss something else. Could we have an additional day to refine the report?"

Sharma's eyes narrowed, his frustration evident. "More time? Ram, we're already on a tight schedule. The client is expecting this by evening today."

Trying to remain calm, Ram continued, "I know, sir. But we want to deliver something that meets the client's expectations. A few more hours could make all the difference."

Sharma's expression hardened, his voice rising with irritation. "I need a way, not an excuse! We don't have the luxury of time. The client is counting on us, and I expected you two to deliver."

Ram's heart sank, but before he could respond, Priya stepped in. "Mr. Sharma, I agree that we need to deliver on time, but I also believe that if we go into the meeting with this report, we'll be setting ourselves up for failure. We've identified the gaps and know how to fix them, but doing it right will take a bit more time."

Sharma's gaze shifted to Priya, his irritation still simmering. "And what do you suggest, Priya? That we simply tell the client we're not ready?"

Priya met his gaze steadily, choosing her words carefully. "Not at all, sir. I suggest we take this extra time to ensure we present something that meets and exceeds their expectations.

If we can buy just 24 hours, we can deliver a report that we're all proud of and, more importantly, one that secures the client's confidence in us."

Sharma leaned back in his chair, his fingers drumming on the desk. He was silent for a long moment, weighing the situation. The frustration in his eyes softened slightly as he considered Priya's words.

Finally, he nodded, albeit reluctantly. "Alright. I'll ask the client if we can postpone the meeting by 24 hours. But listen carefully—this is your last chance. I expect nothing short of perfection in that report. No more excuses, understood?"

Ram and Priya both nodded, relief washing over them. "Thank you, Sir," Priya said earnestly. "We won't let you down."

Sharma gave a curt nod. "You'd better not. Now get to work. You need to present the revised version to the client tomorrow morning. "

With the clock ticking, Priya and Ram raced to address the issues Sharma had pointed out. They burned the midnight oil, revisiting their data, reworking the narrative, and trying to infuse the report with the needed depth. But despite their efforts, they couldn't shake the feeling that something was still missing.

As the clock ticked 1 AM, exhaustion began to take its toll. They had done all they could but knew more was needed deep down. The client meeting was looming, and the pressure was building.

This was just the beginning of their journey—a journey that would test not just their skills but their resolve, creativity, and ability to think beyond the tools they had learned to rely on.

Ram and Priya walked into the client's boardroom the following day with anticipation and trepidation.

They had spent hours refining their presentation, hoping their reliance on AI tools would pay off. But as they began to present, it quickly became apparent that something was wrong.

The client's expressions were stoic, their feedback was curt, and the room felt cold despite the warm air conditioning.

As the presentation concluded, the client's lead executive, Mr. Atul, sighed and leaned back in his chair. 'Thank you for your efforts,' he said, choosing his words carefully. 'But I must be honest, this isn't what we expected. The data is there but lacks the strategic insight and human touch we need to make informed decisions. We'll have to revisit this.'

Back at the office, Ram and Priya were called into their boss's office. Sharma was uncharacteristically stern. 'I just got off the phone with the client,' he began, not bothering with pleasantries. 'They're giving us one more chance, but they were obvious—if we don't deliver something exceptional in the next 30 days, we lose the account.'

Ram and Priya exchanged worried glances. They knew what this meant. This account was crucial for the company, and losing it would have significant repercussions—not just for the business but their careers.

'You have 15 days,' Sharma continued. '15 days to turn this around. I don't need to tell you what's at stake here. You can do it, but you need to figure out where you went wrong and fix it. No excuses.'

Chapter 2

The weight of expectations

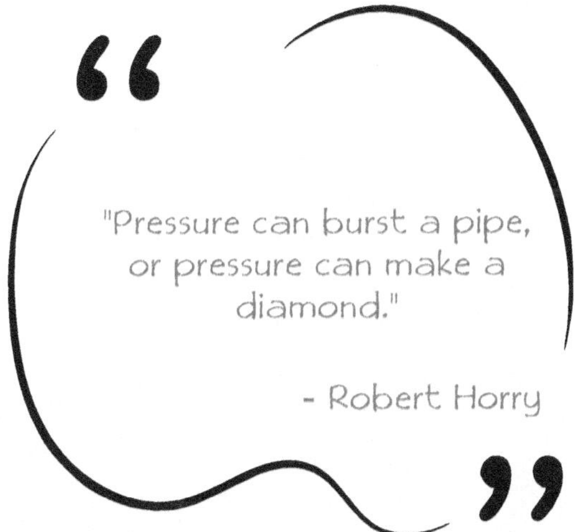

The gravity of the situation settled over them like a heavy cloud. They had no choice but to accept the ultimatum, even though they felt the pressure mounting. As they left Mr. Sharma's office, the reality of their predicament began to sink in. They have 15 days to redeem themselves—or face the consequences.

The sun was just beginning to rise, casting a pale glow over the city, but inside the ClickFlix office, the atmosphere was anything but serene.

Priya and Ram sat in silence, their eyes heavy with fatigue, staring at their screens. The clock read 7:00 AM, and the reality of the day ahead was starting to sink in. Sharma's words echoed in their minds: 'Fix this, or face the consequences.'

The pressure was unlike anything they had faced before. This wasn't just about delivering a project; it was about their careers, their reputations, and the future of ClickFlix's relationship with its most important client. The weight of expectations hung heavily on their shoulders, and every passing minute felt like an eternity.

Priya glanced at Ram, who was frantically typing away, trying to find the right words to salvage their report. 'What if we don't make it?' she thought, a knot forming in her stomach. The fear of failure was gnawing at her confidence, and for the first time, she began to doubt whether they could pull this off.

Ram was feeling the same pressure. He had always been the calm and collected one, but today, his nerves were frayed. The more he thought about the gaps in their report, the more he realized how much they had underestimated the task.

They had relied too much on AI, assuming it would do the heavy lifting, but they had neglected the human element— the critical thinking, the creativity, the storytelling that Atul was expecting.

'We're running out of time,' Ram muttered, breaking the silence. 'We need to come up with something that will impress Atul, something that shows we understand his needs and can deliver real value.'

Priya nodded, but the exhaustion was making it hard to think clearly. 'Maybe we need to take a step back,' she suggested. 'We've been so focused on the data and the tools, but we're missing the bigger picture. Maybe we need to approach this from a different angle.'

They both knew that they needed help, but who could they turn to? Sharma had made it clear that this was their responsibility, and there was no room for error. But as the clock ticked closer to the client meeting, Priya's mind drifted to a conversation she had with an old colleague weeks ago. 'Rishi,' she whispered, almost to herself.

Ram looked up, confused. 'Rishi? Who's that?' he asked.

'He's someone who might be able to help us,' Priya explained. 'He used to be in the corporate world, a leader in this field, but he left it all behind. He's turned inward, focusing on spiritual growth, but he knows more about these challenges than anyone I've ever met.'

'Are you sure he'll help us?' Ram asked, skepticism creeping into his voice.

'I don't know,' Priya admitted. 'He's not exactly the mentoring type anymore, and I've heard he can be difficult, but at this point, what do we have to lose? If we don't find a way to turn this around, we're finished.'

With no other options in sight, Ram agreed. They decided to reach out to Rishi, hoping against hope that he would agree to help them. But deep down, they both knew that convincing Rishi to mentor them wouldn't be easy.

They were about to face a new kind of challenge—one that would test not only their professional skills but also their determination, humility, and willingness to learn.

As they prepared to reach out to Rishi, a sense of unease settled over them.

They had no idea what to expect, but they knew that whatever happened next would be a turning point in their journey.

The weight of expectations was heavy, but they were ready to face it head-on, even if it meant confronting their own shortcomings.

<table><tr><td>**Chapter**
3</td><td>**The mentor's call**</td></tr></table>

Guidance from the Unlikely Hero

Now fueled by desperation and determination, Priya and Ram decided to reach out to Rishi. The following day, they traveled to the city's outskirts, where Rishi had retreated to a quiet, secluded life. As they drove, the anxiety in the car was palpable. Priya had only heard about Rishi's temperamental nature but had no idea what to expect in person.

The road wound through dense forests, the trees closing in around them as they climbed higher into the hills. Ram, usually the more grounded of the two, couldn't help but feel a sense of foreboding. 'Are you sure this is the right place?' he asked, glancing at the GPS, which was starting to lose signal.

'It has to be,' Priya replied, though her voice betrayed her uncertainty. 'Rishi is known for his reclusive lifestyle.

He left the corporate world behind for a reason. We have to hope he's willing to listen to us.'

They finally arrived at a modern, double-storied, glass-cladded cottage tucked away among the trees. The only sounds were the rustle of leaves and the distant chirping of birds. As they approached the door, Priya hesitated for a moment before knocking. The door creaked open slightly, revealing a man in his mid-fifties with sharp eyes and a no-nonsense expression. This was Rishi.

'What do you want?' Rishi's voice was terse, matching his stern demeanor. He eyed them suspiciously as if he already knew the answer but was testing their resolve.

Torn aback by the abrupt greeting, Ram struggled to find the right words. 'We… we need your help,' he finally managed to say. 'We've hit a wall with our project and don't know how to move forward.'

'Help?' Rishi scoffed, clearly unimpressed. 'You come all the way here because you've hit a wall? And you think I'm just going to solve your problems for you?'

Priya stepped forward, trying to keep her voice steady. 'We're not asking for easy answers,' she said. 'We've already put in the work, but we realize now that we've missed something crucial. We've let AI think for us, and it's backfired. We need your guidance to figure out what we're doing wrong.'

Rishi's eyes narrowed as he studied them both. There was a long, uncomfortable silence before he finally spoke. 'Most people who come to me are looking for shortcuts, but you don't strike me as the type to give up easily,' he said, more to himself than to them.
 'I left the corporate world because I was tired of the shallowness, the lack of depth in how people approached problems. But maybe, just maybe, you're different.'

'I'll help you,' Rishi continued, his tone softening slightly, 'but on my terms. I'm not going to spoon-feed you with solutions. If you're willing to learn, to dig deep and confront your weaknesses, then we can begin.'

Relief washed over Priya and Ram, but it was tempered by the realization that this would not be an easy journey. They nodded in agreement, ready to accept whatever challenges lay ahead.

Rishi invited them into his home, which was simple and uncluttered, a reflection of the man himself. He wasted no time in getting to the point. 'Show me your report,' he said, motioning for them to set up their laptops.

As they walked Rishi through their project, pointing out the data they had analyzed and the AI-generated insights, he listened carefully, his expression unreadable. When they finished, there was another long pause before Rishi spoke.

'You've been relying too much on shortcuts,' Rishi said firmly. 'AI, templates, formulas—those things can be useful, but they've become a crutch for you. You've forgotten how to think critically and how to approach a problem with fresh eyes. That's why you failed.'

Priya, still stung by the criticism they had received from the client, asked, 'But how do we handle it when the feedback is so harsh? It's hard not to take it personally.'

Rishi paused, considering her words. 'Criticism is a tool, Priya,' he said finally. 'It's not about you, it's about the work. If you take it personally, you're missing the point. Instead, use it to fuel your improvement. Ask yourself: What can I learn from this? How can I use this to get better? That's how you turn criticism into growth.'

Ram had his own concerns. 'We're under so much pressure to deliver results quickly. It's stifling creativity in the team. How do we foster innovation when we're constantly up against deadlines?'

Rishi leaned back, a slight smile playing on his lips. 'Pressure is part of the job, Ram. But creativity isn't about having endless time; it's about making the most of the time you have. Start by setting aside short bursts of time for brainstorming—creative sprints. No judgment, no filters, just ideas. Then, prioritize quickly and assign ownership. Creativity thrives when it's given direction, not when it's left to drift.'

As they delved deeper into their challenges, Priya brought up another issue that had been weighing on her mind. 'There's been no balance in my life, Rishi. It's all work, and I'm exhausted. How do I manage everything without burning out?'

Rishi's gaze softened slightly. 'Balance is about boundaries, Priya. You need to decide what matters most and protect that. Define your priorities and then set clear boundaries around them. And don't be afraid to reassess those boundaries regularly. As for burnout—focus on the process, not just the outcome. Celebrate your efforts, not just your successes. That's how you stay motivated and avoid burning out.'

Rishi began to deconstruct their report, pointing out not just the flaws, but the missed opportunities. He explained the importance of storytelling in business, of connecting data to real-world applications. 'A good report isn't just about accuracy,' he said. 'It's about impact. You need to weave a narrative that makes the client see the value in your work. AI can help you gather information, but it's your job to turn that information into a compelling story.'

He didn't give them answers, but instead asked probing questions that forced them to think deeply about their approach. 'Why should Atul trust you with this project?' he asked. 'How are you demonstrating respect for his needs? What are you contributing beyond what the AI has generated?'

The hours that followed were grueling. Rishi was relentless, pushing Ram and Priya far beyond their comfort zones. He dissected their previous work with ruthless precision, pointing out every flaw, every missed opportunity. It was a humbling experience, but it was also exactly what they needed.

Through these conversations, Ram and Priya began to understand that the solutions to their problems weren't in some external tool or strategy—they were within themselves. Rishi wasn't just teaching them how to fix their presentation; he was teaching them how to fix their approach to work, to leadership, and to life.

Under Rishi's guidance, they began to see the cracks in their approach—not just in the presentation they had created, but in the way they had been approaching their work for years.

By the end of the session, Priya and Ram were exhausted, but they also felt a renewed sense of purpose. Rishi had given them a lot to think about, and they knew that the road ahead would be tough. But for the first time in days, they felt like they were moving in the right direction.

Chapter 4

Shattered confidence

Facing the Reality of Failure

Priya and Ram left Rishi's cottage late in the evening, their minds reeling from the intense session. The weight of his words hung over them like a dark cloud. They had come seeking answers, but instead, they were confronted with more questions—questions that cut to the core of their approach, their skills, and their very understanding of what it took to succeed.

'I thought we were doing everything right,' Priya said, breaking the silence as they drove back to the city. 'We followed the steps, used the tools, and yet, it wasn't enough.'

Ram nodded, his eyes fixed on the road. 'Rishi made it clear that we've been too reliant on AI, but it's not just that. We haven't been thinking critically. We've been so focused on getting the task done that we've lost sight of the bigger picture.'

'What if we're not cut out for this?' Priya's voice trembled slightly, revealing the insecurity that had been growing inside her. 'What if we can't figure this out, even with Rishi's help?'

'We have to,' Ram replied, though he didn't sound entirely convinced. 'Sharma's ultimatum isn't going away, and the client meeting is in just a few days. We don't have a choice.'

When they returned to the office the next morning, the atmosphere was tense. Their colleagues could sense that something was wrong, but no one dared to ask. Priya and Ram went straight to work, trying to apply the lessons Rishi had imparted.

But as the hours passed, frustration set in. Every time they tried to rework the report, they found themselves second-guessing their decisions. The confidence they once had in their AI-driven insights was shattered. Now, every piece of data, every conclusion they drew felt suspect, as if they were fumbling in the dark.

'How do we know if we're getting it right?' Priya asked, staring at her screen, the cursor blinking accusingly at her. 'Rishi gave us principles, but he didn't tell us how to apply them exactly. What if we're just making things worse?'

Ram sighed, running a hand through his hair. 'We've been trained to rely on AI, on data, but now we have to think beyond that. We have to infuse this report with the human element, with the story that Rishi talked about. But how do we do that when we've never had to before?'

The breaking point came late in the afternoon. After hours of work, they had a new draft, but it still didn't feel right. Priya slammed her laptop shut in frustration. 'This isn't working, Ram! We're just spinning our wheels. Maybe we're not cut out for this after all.'

'Don't say that,' Ram shot back, though his own resolve was crumbling. 'We've come this far. We can't give up now. Maybe... maybe we need to talk to Rishi again. Maybe we missed something.'

'But what if he just tells us the same thing?' Priya asked, her voice tinged with despair. 'What if we're just not good enough to do this, Ram?'

Ram didn't have an answer. All he knew was that they were running out of time, and they needed to find a way forward. 'Let's give it one more shot. We'll go back to Rishi, but this time, we won't leave until we understand exactly what we need to do.'

With heavy hearts and uncertain minds, Priya and Ram prepared to make the journey back to Rishi's cottage. They were tired, defeated, and their confidence was in tatters. But somewhere deep inside, a small spark of determination remained.

They had to get this right—not just for Sharma or the client, but for themselves. The journey was far from over, and the toughest challenges were still ahead.

Chapter 5

Rise from the ashes

"The phoenix must burn to emerge."

-Janet Fitch

The path to Rishi's cottage was quiet, with only the sound of the wind rustling through the trees. Priya and Ram walked side by side, their steps slow and deliberate.

The initial session with Rishi had been anything but easy—his sharp critiques and demanding nature had left them both feeling bruised. Yet, after days of wrestling with the challenges ahead, they realized they had no choice but to

seek his guidance once more.

As they reached the door of the modest cottage, Ram hesitated, glancing at Priya. "Are we sure about this? The last session was… intense. What if he's even tougher on us this time?"
Priya took a deep breath, nodding. "I've thought about it a lot. We don't have any other options, Ram. If we want to succeed, we need someone who's going to push us. Rishi's the only one who can do that."

Ram sighed but nodded in agreement. "You're right. Let's do this."

They knocked on the door, the sound echoing in the stillness. After a moment, the door creaked open, and there stood Rishi, his expression unreadable.

"Back again?" Rishi said, his voice calm but with an edge of curiosity. "I wasn't sure I'd see you two so soon."

Priya stepped forward, her voice steady but tinged with uncertainty. "We need your help, Rishi. We know the last session was rough, but we've realized that we can't do this without you. Will you mentor us?"

Rishi knew that Ram and Priya would return. He knew that were now ready to dive deeper. The time had come for them to face the tough questions—the questions that would force them to confront their own weaknesses, assumptions, and fears.

Rishi's gaze shifted between them, his eyes narrowing slightly. "Mentorship isn't something I offer lightly. The last time we met, I wasn't convinced that you were fully committed. You both have potential, but potential means nothing without the willingness to work hard—without shortcuts."

Ram swallowed, remembering how brutally honest Rishi had been during their last encounter. "We understand that, Rishi. We're ready to commit fully this time. No shortcuts, no excuses."

Rishi crossed his arms, studying them carefully. "If I agree to mentor you, there are conditions. First, you need to be serious—no half-hearted attempts. This will require discipline, focus, and a willingness to be uncomfortable. Growth doesn't come from comfort zones."

Priya nodded earnestly. "We understand, Rishi. We're prepared to do whatever it takes."

Rishi continued, his tone firm. "Second, there will be no shortcuts. You'll need to apply what you learn thoroughly and methodically. If you're looking for quick fixes, you're wasting your time—and mine."

Ram and Priya exchanged a look, both of them knowing that they were ready to accept the challenge.

"We agree to your conditions, Rishi," Ram said, his voice filled with determination. "We're ready to learn, and we'll do it the right way."

Rishi uncrossed his arms, nodding slightly. "Good. Then we'll start your first session tomorrow morning at sunrise. Be here on time, and be prepared to work."
Priya and Ram both nodded, feeling a mix of nerves and excitement. They knew the road ahead would be tough, but with Rishi's guidance, they also knew they had a real chance at success.

"Thank you, Rishi," Priya said sincerely. "We won't let you down."
Rishi gave a small, almost imperceptible smile. "We'll see about that. Get some rest—you'll need it. I will see you tomorrow morning at 6 AM"

As they left the cottage, the weight of their decision settled over them, but so did a newfound sense of determination. They had chosen the harder path, but they were ready to face it head-on.

Section 2

The Core of Transformation

Chapter 6

Forged in the fire

> **"Do not pray for an easy life, pray for the strength to endure a difficult one."**
>
> — Bruce Lee

Getting ready

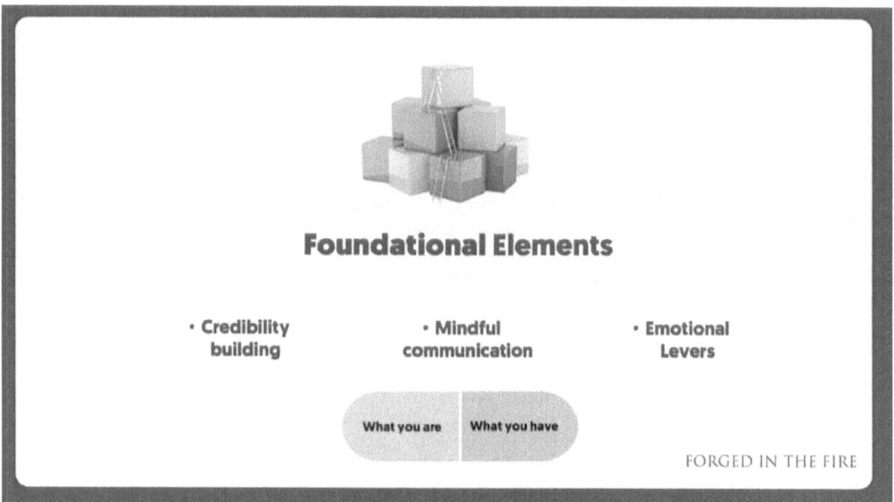

As agreed, Priya and Ram reached Rishi's home well before 6 AM. The sun barely rose, casting a soft golden light over Rishi's cottage. The air was cool and crisp, starkly contrasting the nervous energy that Priya and Ram felt as they approached the front steps.

The weight of the day ahead pressed down on them, but they were determined to face whatever Rishi had in store.

Rishi was already outside, waiting for them. He stood with his arms crossed, his expression as unreadable as ever. As they walked up, he nodded slightly, acknowledging their punctuality.

"Good. You're on time," Rishi said, his voice low but commanding. "That's the first step. But being here isn't enough. Today, we're going to set some ground rules."

Priya and Ram stood at attention, their anticipation growing with every word.

Rishi continued, his gaze intense. "Before we dive into the work, you need to understand something crucial. You're not just here to fix a report or impress a client. If that's all you're aiming for, you'll fail again. The stakes are higher than that."

Ram frowned slightly, the weight of Rishi's words sinking in. "What do you mean, Rishi?"

Rishi looked directly at him, his eyes piercing. "You failed in your last attempt not because you lacked tools or resources, but because you didn't fully understand what it takes to succeed—not just in this project, but in your careers, and even in your lives."

Priya shifted uncomfortably, the truth in Rishi's words cutting deep. "We thought we were prepared. We used the tools we had, but... clearly, it wasn't enough."

Rishi nodded, his tone softening slightly. "Exactly. It's not enough to just use the tools at your disposal. You need to understand them, master them, and most importantly, know when and how to apply them. But it goes deeper than that."

He paused, letting the silence underscore his next point. "Success isn't just about doing the work. It's about knowing yourself, understanding your weaknesses, and having the discipline to turn those weaknesses into strengths. It's about seeing the bigger picture, about what it will take to not only succeed in this project but to build a career and a life that you're proud of."

Ram and Priya exchanged a glance, the gravity of Rishi's words settling over them. This wasn't just about fixing a mistake—it was about changing the way they approached everything.

Rishi continued, his voice steady. "The ground rules are simple: be honest with yourselves, commit fully to this process, and be willing to confront uncomfortable truths. You'll need to work harder than you ever have, but if you're serious about this, you'll come out stronger—both as professionals and as individuals."

Priya took a deep breath, her resolve hardening. "We're ready, Rishi. We want to learn, to grow, and to do whatever it takes to succeed."

Ram nodded in agreement. "We'll follow your lead. No shortcuts, no excuses."

Rishi gave a slight nod of approval. "Good. Then let's get started. The first thing we'll do is dissect where you went wrong. Understanding your failure is the key to unlocking your success. Only by confronting it head-on can you hope to avoid the same mistakes in the future."

With that, Rishi turned and led them into the cottage, the morning light casting long shadows behind them.

Priya and Ram had been anticipating this moment since they arrived at Rishi's cottage. Both of them are fully aware that this was the beginning of a journey that would test them in ways they had never imagined. As they followed Rishi down the hallway, they couldn't help but feel a mix of curiosity and excitement about what awaited them.

When Rishi finally opened the door to his private home-office, the sight that greeted them was a striking blend of old-world wisdom and cutting-edge technology.

The room was bathed in soft natural light, filtered through smart glass windows that could adjust their opacity with a simple voice command. Shelves lined the walls, filled to the brim with books that spanned centuries of knowledge—ancient texts on philosophy and spirituality sat alongside the latest bestsellers on leadership, psychology, and technology.

There was a separate shelf dedicated to place the books Rishi had authored along with the medals and mementos he received.

On the far wall, a massive digital screen seamlessly integrated with the room's decor, displaying a rotating selection of motivational quotes, real-time data feeds, and images of breathtaking landscapes. A sleek, minimalist desk stood in the center, dominated by a state-of-the-art laptop, wireless charging pads, and a multi-device docking station.

The desk itself was a marvel of modern engineering, adjustable in height and angle, controlled by Rishi's voice or gestures.

As they entered, Rishi swiped his hand over a touchpad embedded in the wall, and the room seemed to come alive. The smart glass windows darkened slightly to reduce glare, while a soft ambient light adjusted to provide perfect visibility. The digital screen transitioned to display a serene scene of a mountain range, adding a calming effect to the room.

Priya noticed a set of virtual reality headsets neatly arranged on a side table, next to a small meditation altar adorned with simple yet elegant artifacts. It was a juxtaposition that seemed to perfectly capture Rishi's dual nature—a man deeply rooted in spirituality, yet fully embracing the advancements of modern technology.

Ram's eyes were drawn to a corner of the room where a bookshelf was dedicated entirely to the latest gadgets— drones, smart speakers, and even a few pieces of AI-driven home automation devices. It was clear that Rishi didn't just dabble in technology; he was deeply invested in understanding and utilizing it to its fullest potential.

Rishi gestured for them to take a seat in the ergonomic chairs arranged in front of the desk. As they did, they couldn't help but feel a sense of awe at how effortlessly Rishi had integrated the most advanced technology with his pursuit of deeper wisdom.

"This room," Rishi began, noticing their fascination, "is a reflection of my belief that technology and spirituality are not at odds—they can, in fact, complement each other beautifully. The key is to use technology mindfully, as a tool to enhance our understanding, productivity, and connection to the world around us."

He paused, letting his words sink in. "As we go through today's session, you'll see how these tools can help us not just in work, but in living a more meaningful, informed, and balanced life."

Priya and Ram nodded, eager to begin. They were beginning to understand that Rishi was not just a mentor in leadership, but also in how to harmonize the advances of the modern world with timeless wisdom.

As the room settled into a comfortable silence, Rishi looked at Priya and Ram with a thoughtful expression. They had come a long way in their journey, but Rishi knew that the true test of their leadership would come when they applied the skills they were about to learn. He wanted to set the stage, to prepare them for the deep dive into the frameworks that would transform their approach to leadership, communication, and team management.

Rishi leaned forward, his voice calm but filled with purpose. "Before we dive into the specifics, I want to give you a clear picture of what we're going to cover. These skills and frameworks are the building blocks of effective leadership and communication. They're not just techniques—they're mindsets that will shape how you approach every challenge and opportunity."

Priya and Ram exchanged curious glances, sensing that they were about to uncover something truly transformative. "First," Rishi continued, "**we'll explore the Foundational Skills.**

These are the core principles that underpin everything you do as a leader. They include:

1. A framework covering the **qualities that make a leader trustworthy and inspirational.** Authenticity, Credibility, Contribution, Respect, Empathy, Dedication, Integrity, Inspiration, and Trustworthiness—these are the traits that will earn you the respect and loyalty of your team.

2. A method for **creating an environment where your team can thrive.**

3. A method **to guide you in practicing clear and mindful communication.** These skills will ensure that your communication is clear, thoughtful, and effective.

Rishi paused, letting the weight of these foundational skills sink in. "These are the skills that will define your character as a leader. They're about who you are and how you interact with others."

Ram nodded slowly, understanding the importance of building a strong foundation. "What comes next?"

"Once you've mastered the foundational skills," Rishi continued, "we move on to Methods Used for Organizing. Leadership is not just about guiding people—it's about organizing your time, tasks, and resources effectively. These methods include:

1. I will introduce you to a framework will **help you focus on what truly matters**. It's about identifying your key objectives, organizing tasks by urgency and importance, and managing your time effectively to achieve your goals.

2. We will then move to a framework that **helps you manage change within your team or organization**. It's about clear communication, handling resistance, aligning with the broader vision, and ensuring a smooth transition."

Priya leaned in, eager to learn. "**And what about communication? We've struggled with both written and oral communication in the past.**"

Rishi smiled, anticipating the question. "That's why we'll spend a significant amount of time on proven methods used for written and oral communication. These are crucial for conveying your ideas clearly and persuasively, whether in writing or in conversation.

For written communication, we'll cover:

1. A method about **presenting your thoughts persuasively**, profiling your audience, engaging them with stories, and ending with a strong call to action.

2. A solid framework that teaches you **how to structure your message** in a way that resonates emotionally setting the stage, triggering conflict, outlining the journey, revealing the resolution, and highlighting the key takeaway.

3. A simple method **to guide you in writing clear and concise messages** that are logical, engaging, accurate, and responsive.

4. Another framework about **making your reports and presentations insightful, focusing on data-driven decisions,** synthesizing information, and generating actionable insights."

Priya's eyes lit up with excitement. "That sounds exactly like what we need."

Rishi nodded, pleased with their enthusiasm. "**For oral communication**, we'll dive into:

1. A method about **effective team collaboration**—connecting, organizing, aligning, leveraging strengths, engaging, supporting, and evaluating.

2. Another foundational **aspect to master the layers of communication**—listening, assessing, yielding, engaging, and responding.

3. A simple **guide to non-verbal communication**—showing confident body language, interpreting others' cues, using gestures purposefully, neutralizing negative signals, aligning with your verbal messages, and listening attentively."

Ram leaned back, absorbing the breadth of what they were about to learn. "It sounds like these skills will cover every aspect of communication."

"They will," Rishi confirmed. "And finally, we'll cover various key methods you can use in special and complex situations. These methods used for team management, bonding, problem-solving, conflict resolution, negotiation, and tough conversations.

These are the skills that will help you navigate the complexities of leading a team, especially when things get tough:

1. A framework for **problem-solving**—setting the stage, separating people from the problem, overcoming biases, learning about the problem, visualizing alternatives, executing the plan, and reflecting on the outcomes.

2. Another one about **resolving conflicts** and reaching consensus—starting with commitment, appreciating the opposite perspective, identifying needs, finding common ground, unifying views, and resolving the issue.

3. One more framework is for **supporting your team through challenges**—hearing them out, empathizing, assuring them of solutions, liberating them from pains, and evaluating the process.

4. Another guide to **effective negotiation**—navigating needs, evaluating options, finding common ground, adapting, and tying up agreements.

5. One powerful concept about **mediating conflicts**—bringing parties together, exploring issues, discussing openly, identifying solutions, agreeing on terms, and ensuring implementation.

6. A critical framework **for handling tough conversations**—clarifying the purpose, respecting emotions, understanding perspectives, communicating clearly, finding common ground, and agreeing on actions.

7. A variant of the above framework for **managing sensitive issues**—defining the issue, empathizing with emotions, listening actively, informing with clarity, collaborating on solutions, and evaluating the outcome."

Rishi continued. "**Along with these skills, you need to learn how to balance emotional and rational sides and pick up some resilience.** Therefore, I will cover the following:

1. Emotional Intelligence
2. Critical Thinking
3. Resilience

Rishi paused, looking at Priya and Ram with a sense of pride. "These frameworks are not just tools—they're a mindset. They're about leading with empathy, clarity, and purpose. If you master these, you'll be equipped to handle any challenge that comes your way."

Priya and Ram exchanged determined glances. They knew that what they were about to learn would transform not only their approach to leadership but also their entire careers.

Rishi leaned back, his tone intensifying as he spoke. "Before all of these It's essential to establish trust and credibility before anyone will listen to you, let alone follow you. Without these, no amount of tactical communication will work. Trust is the bedrock of any successful team."

6.1 Foundational Elements

6.1.1 Being an ACCREDIITed leader

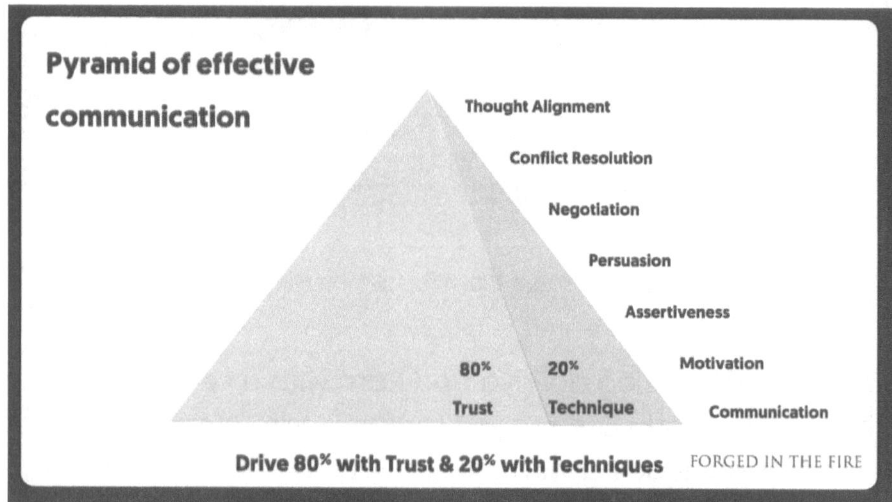

"We will cover Trust in different ways" Rishi highlighted the importance of Trust and continued "It's essential for you know that Trust drives 80% of the communication."

Priya, confident but almost defensive, said, "But Rishi, our team trusts us. We've been working together for a while now, and I believe they trust our leadership."

Rishi's gaze cut through Priya's confidence like a knife. "Do they really trust you, Priya? Or do they just comply with your directives? When was the last time they came to you for guidance without hesitation? And how do you demonstrate integrity and authenticity in your day-to-day leadership?"

Priya hesitated, doubt creeping in for the first time. She realized that trust might not be as solid as she had assumed.

Breaking the silence, Ram voiced the question that had been gnawing at both of them. "Rishi, how do we find out the true intentions of our team members? And what qualities naturally draw a team to their leader?"

Rishi nodded, pleased with the direction of the conversation. "These are the right questions, Ram. To lead effectively, you need to build a foundation of trust and credibility. Let me explain the first method. It will give you a clear starting path."

He paused for a moment, ensuring they were fully engaged, then continued. "As a leader, you are expected to demonstrate nine key qualities. These aren't arbitrary; they are fundamental."

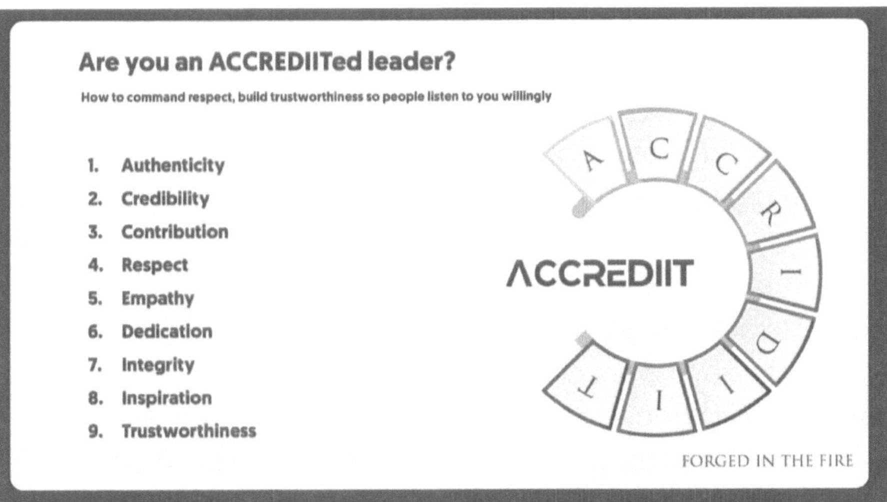

Are you an ACCREDIITed leader?

How to command respect, build trustworthiness so people listen to you willingly

1. Authenticity
2. Credibility
3. Contribution
4. Respect
5. Empathy
6. Dedication
7. Integrity
8. Inspiration
9. Trustworthiness

Authenticity: When a leader is authentic, they foster an environment of openness and trust. Team members feel comfortable being themselves, leading to higher engagement and stronger relationships. Inauthenticity creates skepticism. Team members may question the leader's motives, leading to disengagement and resistance.

Credibility: A credible leader is viewed as a reliable source of knowledge and wisdom. This ensures that their guidance is followed and their decisions are respected. Without credibility, a leader's ability to influence is severely diminished. Team members may disregard their instructions, leading to chaos and inefficiency.

Contribution: A contributing leader actively enhances team performance, bringing fresh ideas and driving progress. A passive leader who contributes little can lead to stagnation. The team may lack direction and motivation, reducing overall productivity.

Respect: Respectful leaders build strong, collaborative teams. People feel valued, leading to a positive work culture and enhanced performance. Disrespect breeds resentment and conflict, making teamwork difficult and reducing overall morale.

Empathy: Empathetic leaders create supportive environments where team members feel understood and valued. This leads to stronger bonds and increased loyalty. A lack of empathy can make team members feel isolated and unappreciated, increasing stress and turnover rates.

Dedication: Dedicated leaders are seen as reliable and committed. Their persistence encourages the team to remain focused and resilient in the face of challenges. Without dedication, a leader's unreliability can cause missed deadlines and a lack of progress, damaging the team's effectiveness.

Integrity: Integrity ensures that a leader's actions are consistent with ethical standards, fostering trust and a positive reputation. Ethical lapses can lead to significant fallout, including loss of trust, legal consequences, and a damaged organizational culture.

Inspiration: Inspirational leaders ignite passion and creativity within their teams, driving innovation and sustained effort. Without inspiration, the team may become complacent, lacking the drive to excel or pursue ambitious goals.

Trustworthiness: A trustworthy leader builds a foundation of reliability and transparency. Team members feel secure and are more likely to be open and communicative. When trust is absent, the team's foundation crumbles. Miscommunication and mistrust lead to dysfunction and a breakdown in collaboration.

Priya looked a bit overwhelmed. 'That's a lot to take in, Rishi. How are we supposed to remember all of this?'

Rishi smiled reassuringly. 'That's precisely why I've put these qualities in a sequence that forms the acronym ACCREDIIT. It's not just a mnemonic; it's a framework that you can actively apply to your leadership style.'

Priya and Ram were thrilled to hear the new acronym that's going to make them authentic and trustworthy leaders. The framework is apt and easy to remember. Both of them realised that they could be falling short of one or more of these nine qualities and there is lot of room for improvement.

"Once you embody these qualities," Rishi concluded, "your communication will naturally be more effective. But first, you must internalize these principles and let them guide every action and decision you make."

Ram and Priya listened intently, realizing the depth of what Rishi was teaching them. They had been so focused on the mechanics of communication that they had overlooked the critical foundation—being the kind of leaders people wanted to follow.

Priya nodded her head affirmatively and recapped her new learning: "I get it now. The first step is to get accredited. But I don't mean in the traditional sense of certifications or titles. This is something much deeper.'

Ram could not contain his ecstasy after identifying the potential blind spot. He leaned forward and said "Yes these nine qualities make us ACCREDIITed leaders!"

Rishi leaned forward, his eyes widening. ' Yes. ACCREDIIT is a framework—a way of thinking and being that ensures you are not just doing the right things, but that you are the right kind of person to be doing them. These are not just traits; they are the foundation of leadership and success. Without them, any success you achieve will be hollow and unsustainable.'

"These are the qualities that will make people see you as credible leaders, and together, I call them 'ACCREDIIT'. It's an acronym that will help you remember these principles easily, but don't mistake them for just words. They are the essence of effective leadership."

"Let's go through them one by one. First, Authenticity," Rishi said, his voice steady. "When you're authentic, you foster an environment of openness and trust. Team members feel comfortable being themselves, which leads to higher engagement and stronger relationships. But if you're inauthentic, people will sense it.

They may begin to question your motives, leading to disengagement and resistance."

Priya nodded slowly, a realization dawning on her. "So, it's not just about being true to others but being true to ourselves as well."

"Exactly," Rishi affirmed. "Authenticity starts with self-awareness and extends to how you interact with others. It's the first step in building genuine relationships."

Ram, still processing, frowned slightly. "What about credibility? I get that it's about building trust, but isn't credibility earned over time? How do we establish it quickly, especially when we're under pressure like we are now?"

Rishi leaned forward, his eyes locking onto Ram's. "Credibility is indeed built over time, but it starts with your first interaction. It's about demonstrating competence, integrity, and honesty from the get-go. When you say you'll do something, follow through. Be transparent about challenges.

Even if things don't go as planned, being upfront about it actually enhances your credibility because people see that you're honest and trustworthy."

Rishi continued, "Credibility is earned through consistent competence, integrity, and honesty. It starts with small, everyday actions—following through on commitments, being transparent about challenges.

Even when things don't go as planned, being upfront about it can enhance your credibility because people see that you're honest and trustworthy."

Ram leaned back, considering this. "But credibility takes time to build. How do we establish it quickly, especially when we're under pressure like we are now?"

"Start with small, consistent actions," Rishi advised. "Follow through on your commitments. Be honest, even when it's uncomfortable. Credibility is built one interaction at a time." Priya's eyes lit up with realization.

"So, if we're transparent with Atul about the challenges we're facing, even if it's not what he wants to hear, that could actually work in our favor?"

"Absolutely," Rishi confirmed. his tone firm. "People value honesty. It's better to be upfront about difficulties than to hide them and risk losing trust later on. Trust me, once you lose credibility, it's very hard to regain."

Ram, still a bit skeptical, pressed on. "And contribution? We're already working hard, contributing as much as we can. How does this fit into the bigger picture?"

Rishi smiled slightly, seeing the gears turning in Ram's mind. "Contribution isn't just about doing your job. It's about adding value in every interaction and inspiring others to do the same.

It's the difference between just completing a task and actively looking for ways to improve the process, to help others succeed, and to push the organization forward. When you contribute meaningfully, it shows that you're invested in more than just your own success—you're invested in the success of the entire team and organization."
Priya's eyes lit up with realization. "So, it's like going beyond what's expected, not just for personal gain but for the greater good of the team?"

"Yes, exactly," Rishi replied, nodding. "Your contribution sets the tone for the entire team. When they see you actively involved, they'll follow suit."

Ram, now deep in thought, said, "Respect and empathy—I understand these in theory, but how do we apply them, especially when we're under so much pressure? It's hard to always be kind and considerate when deadlines are looming."

Rishi nodded understandingly, knowing firsthand the challenges of leadership under pressure. "Pressure can definitely make it challenging to maintain respect and empathy, but that's when they're most important. Respect is about valuing others, even in stressful situations. It means listening, being patient, and treating everyone with kindness, regardless of the circumstances.

Empathy goes a step further—it's about truly understanding and sharing the feelings of others. When you take the time to connect with your team or your clients on an emotional level, you can resolve conflicts more effectively and build stronger relationships."

Priya looked worried. "But what if showing too much empathy makes us seem weak or indecisive?"
Rishi shook his head, his expression serious. "Empathy isn't about being weak—it's about strength. It takes strength to listen, to put yourself in someone else's shoes, and to respond with understanding rather than just reacting. When you lead with empathy, you create a supportive environment where people feel valued and motivated. That's how you build loyalty and trust."

Ram, nodding slowly as the concept sank in, asked, "And dedication—how do we show that without burning out? We're already working so hard."

"Dedication isn't just about working long hours," Rishi explained, his tone reassuring. "It's about being reliable, committed, and showing a strong work ethic. It's about going the extra mile when it's needed but also knowing when to step back and recharge so you can continue to perform at your best.

Dedication is also about being there for your team—showing them that you're in it with them, through thick and thin."

Priya looked more confident now. "I'm starting to see how this all ties together. But what about integrity? We've always tried to be honest and fair, but sometimes the pressure to deliver results makes it hard to uphold those principles."

Rishi's tone was firm as he answered. "Integrity is non-negotiable. It's the cornerstone of everything you do. If you compromise your integrity, even once, it can undo all the trust and credibility you've worked so hard to build. No matter the pressure, always act with honesty and fairness. It might be difficult in the short term, but in the long run, it's what will sustain you and your career."
Ram's voice was serious now, the weight of Rishi's words sinking in. "And inspiration? How do we inspire our team and our client when we're feeling the weight of the world on our shoulders?"

"Inspiration comes from your vision, your enthusiasm, and your ability to motivate others to see beyond the current challenges," Rishi said, his voice rising with energy. "It's about showing people the bigger picture, the potential for success, and energizing them to work towards that vision.

Even when you're under pressure, if you can stay focused on the positive outcomes and communicate that effectively, you'll inspire others to follow your lead."

Priya smiled, feeling more confident. "And trustworthiness... It's about being reliable, transparent, and deserving of trust, right?"

"Exactly," Rishi said, leaning in, his voice steady. "Trust is built over time, but it's maintained through consistency. Be transparent in your actions, follow through on your commitments, and always be someone your team and your clients can rely on, no matter what."

Ram felt a mix of relief and determination as he leaned back. "This is a lot to take in, but it makes sense. We need to embody these values, not just talk about them."

"You've got this," Rishi said, encouragingly. "Remember, ACCREDIIT isn't just a framework—it's a way of leading, a way of living. If you can internalize these values and apply them consistently, you'll not only succeed in this project but in everything you do."

"Rishi," Priya began thoughtfully, "this is all making sense, but I think it would really help us to see the big picture. "
Ram nodded in agreement. "Yeah, we need time to assimilate the information."

Rishi smiled, clearly anticipating their needs. " Let me help you with that. I will show you something that will bring all these elements together."

With a subtle swipe on his smartwatch, Rishi activated the automation in his cottage. The curtains slowly glided shut, dimming the room to a perfect ambiance for a presentation. At the same time, the lights gently adjusted to a soft glow, just enough to keep the room illuminated without overpowering the screen.

Rishi walked over to a sleek, ultra-modern projector sitting discreetly on a shelf. With a simple voice command, he instructed, "Projector on." The device whirred to life, casting a crystal-clear image onto the wall across the room. The infographic that appeared was both elegant and detailed, illustrating the framework in a way that made the concepts immediately accessible.

"This," Rishi said, pointing to the infographic with a laser pointer that seemed to materialize from his smartwatch, "is the visual breakdown of the framework we've been discussing. As you can see, each element is interconnected, forming a cohesive system. Let's walk through it together." Priya leaned forward, her eyes scanning the slide, impressed not only by the clarity of the information but also by the seamless integration of technology. Ram, equally captivated, took out his phone, not to take notes, but to capture the screen for future reference.

Rishi continued, guiding them through the infographic with calm precision. "This visual will help you not only understand each component but also see how they interact with one another. Whenever you feel stuck or need to revisit the concepts, refer back to this visual—it will serve as your roadmap."

As Rishi walked them through each part of the infographic, Priya and Ram felt a newfound clarity. The visual summary pulled everything together, reinforcing their understanding and boosting their confidence in applying what they had learned.

Rishi continued, sensing the growing interest. "Reflect on the following questions"

1. Do you often feel like you have to put on a different persona at work to fit in or be successful?
2. How do you build trust with your team and clients?
3. Are there areas where your credibility could be improved?
4. Are you actively contributing to the growth and success of your organization, or do you find yourself just going through the motions?
5. How do you ensure that you treat everyone with respect, even in stressful situations?

Let's now apply this to a practical scenario. For Example, consider a situation where a project is falling behind schedule due to miscommunication and low morale.

The leader, recognizing the importance of ACCREDIIT, decides to:

- Hold a candid meeting with the team, expressing vulnerability about the challenges they're facing (**Authenticity**).
- Clearly communicate the reasons for the delays and what steps will be taken to get back on track, thereby building trust (**Credibility**).

- Actively engage with the team to find solutions, showing that every contribution matters (**Contribution**).
- Ensure that every team member's concerns are heard and addressed respectfully (**Respect**).
- Take the time to understand the pressures each team member is facing and offer support (**Empathy**).
- Work alongside the team, demonstrating their commitment to overcoming the challenges (**Dedication**).
- Make decisions based on what's right and fair, even if it's difficult (**Integrity**).
- Share a renewed vision for the project, inspiring the team to push through the challenges (**Inspiration**).
- Follow through on all promises and remain transparent throughout the process (**Trustworthiness**).

Ram was curious "Is there an assessment to test all these qualities?"

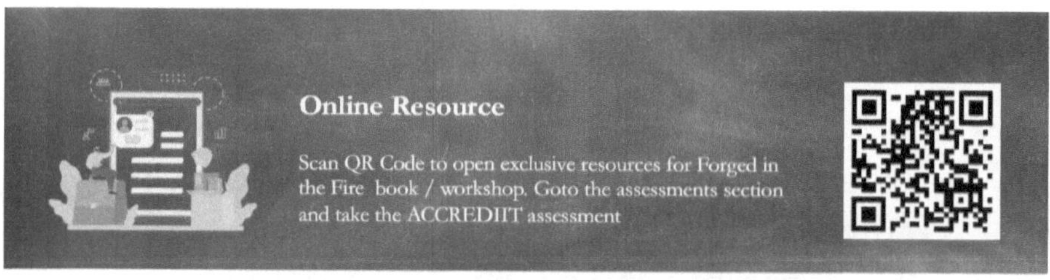

Priya supported his proposal "Yes, it will also help us understand our improvement areas"

Rishi was pleased with their curiosity and responded "Yes. There is a battery of tests. I have developed an assessment for ACCREDIIT. You can take VIA character strengths survey to assess 24 different aspects of your personality. T

he survey goes beyond integrity. I have a ready compendium of all of these on my website and I will give you the access"
Priya and Ram were overjoyed to hear his response and support.

They knew that the next few days would define their careers. But they were delighted to find the support they did not even know they needed badly.

The session continued for 4 hours with several questions by Ram and Priya followed by practical answers from Rishi.
By the end of the session, Ram and Priya felt that they had gained a new perspective on leadership—a perspective that integrated their personal and professional lives, their short-term actions, and long-term aspirations. Rishi's guidance had given them the tools to approach every challenge with clarity, confidence, and integrity.

'Leadership is a journey,' Rishi reminded them as they prepared to leave. **'It's not about perfection; it's about progress. Keep learning, keep growing, and remember that every challenge is an opportunity to become the leader you're meant to be.'**

'But be warned,' Rishi added, his tone growing serious again. 'Partial understanding or failing to embody all these qualities can backfire. Inconsistencies will be noticed, and they can erode the very trust you're trying to build.' Remember, trust is hard to earn but easy to lose.'

He gave examples of leaders who lost credibility by failing to be consistent or by compromising their integrity. Rishi then moved on to prepare them for the next framework.

He paused, letting his words sink in. 'Now that you understand how to establish trust and credibility with ACCREDIIT, it's time to look at how you can create an environment where your team is fully engaged and motivated.

This is where the next framework comes into play.'

Rishi had just finished walking Priya and Ram through the first framework. The discussion had been insightful, and both Priya and Ram were quietly processing the depth of the concepts they had learned.

Authenticity, Credibility, Respect—each element had its own weight, and they knew these principles would shape their future decisions.

Just as Ram was about to ask another question, Rishi glanced at the clock. It was a few minutes past 12 noon.

"Alright, I think that's a good place to pause for now," Rishi said, his voice warm and inviting. "How about we take a break for a brunch? You've earned it."

The suggestion felt like a welcome respite after an intense morning of learning. Priya and Ram both nodded, grateful for the chance to recharge.

"Sounds good," Priya said with a smile. "I could definitely use some food to fuel the brain."

As they made their way to the kitchen, the smell of freshly cooked vegetables and herbs greeted them. The simple yet inviting meal was laid out on the wooden dining table, and Rishi gestured for them to sit.

As they settled into their meal, the conversation naturally turned to Rishi's unique living space. Ram, still fascinated by the technology integrated into the cottage, couldn't resist bringing it up.

"Rishi," Ram began, pausing between bites of his food, "I have to say, the way you've incorporated technology into your home is incredible. Everything's so seamless—the automation, the smart features. It's like a perfect blend of nature and tech."

Priya nodded in agreement, echoing his sentiment. "Yes, it's so subtle but so efficient. You've clearly mastered the balance."

Rishi smiled, setting his glass of water down. "Thank you. I've always believed that technology should serve us without overwhelming us. It's a tool to enhance our lives, not control them."

Ram, curious, leaned forward slightly. "How did you become so tech-savvy? I mean, even though you've shifted your focus to deeper pursuits like spirituality and mentoring, you seem to stay on top of the latest advancements."

Rishi chuckled softly, appreciating the observation. "It's not something that happened overnight. Staying tech-savvy is more about mindset than just knowing how to use the latest gadgets."

He paused for a moment, letting them take that in. "You see, being tech-savvy doesn't mean you need to master every new tool or trend. It's about understanding how technology impacts the world—our work, our relationships, and even our decision-making. You need to stay curious and aware, continuously learning about the advancements that matter."

Priya chimed in, intrigued. "So it's more about having a broader perspective than just diving into one tool or another?"

"Exactly," Rishi replied. "Take Gen AI, for example. It's incredibly powerful, but a leader needs to go beyond using AI tools.

You should also be aware of how technology is reshaping consumer behavior, financial systems, and even global markets. It's about connecting the dots between technological advancements and the real-world changes they bring."

Ram nodded slowly, processing the insight. "So how do you keep up with everything? There's so much out there—it can get overwhelming."

Rishi smiled again. "It's about being selective. You don't need to know everything—just what's relevant to your work, your interests, and your goals.

I make time to read widely, not just about technology but about how it intersects with different industries. Fintech, for example, is something every leader should be familiar with, even if they're not in finance. It's reshaping how we think about money, banking, and consumer habits."

Priya leaned forward, eager to learn more. "And how do you maintain that sense of curiosity and continuous learning?" Rishi took a thoughtful sip. "That's the key, Priya—continuous learning. You never stop. Technology is always evolving, and so should your understanding of it.

The moment you think you've mastered something, it's already outdated. That's why I make it a habit to stay open, to read, to experiment, and to learn from others. And more importantly, I always try to connect the dots between what I know and what I can learn next."

Lunch wrapped up with easy conversation, but the atmosphere shifted slightly as Rishi stood up and motioned for Ram and Priya to follow him. They moved through the cottage to the terrace, where the view of the rolling hills beyond the trees stretched out before them.

A gentle breeze swirled through the air as Rishi poured himself a cup of coffee, the steam rising as he settled into a chair on the terrace. With a practiced hand, he pulled out a small case, revealing a finely rolled cigarette.

Ram followed Rishi outside, curiosity still etched on his face. He admired the serene view but couldn't shake the lingering question from his mind.

Rishi passed on the cigarette packet to Ram and asked him "Do you wish to smoke?" He quickly glanced at Priya and said "Do you mind ?"

Ram politely refused and Priya nodded with a smile.
As Rishi lit the cigarette and took a slow drag, Ram asked, "Rishi, you've given us so much to think about in terms of technology, but what I want to know is—how do you maintain that drive to keep learning? Even now, after everything you've accomplished, you still seem so... driven."

Rishi leaned back in his chair, exhaling smoke into the cool afternoon air. His eyes fixed on the horizon as if contemplating the question deeply before responding.

"Ram, the secret to continuous learning is simple: never get too comfortable. The moment you think you know everything, that's when you stop growing. It doesn't matter how much you've accomplished—what matters is the willingness to keep asking questions, to stay curious about the world around you."

He turned to Ram, his expression serious but kind. "It's not just about learning for work. It's about staying engaged with life. I read books on philosophy, science, technology, even history. I attend webinars, listen to podcasts, and I'm constantly exploring new ideas.

But the most important part of learning is reflection. Taking time to think about what I've learned, to connect it with my experiences, and then using that knowledge to evolve."

Priya, who had followed them to the terrace, chimed in. "So, you're saying it's not just about consuming information but reflecting on it, finding connections, and then applying it in some way?"

Rishi nodded. "Exactly. Continuous learning isn't passive—it's active. It requires you to seek knowledge and then integrate it into your thinking, your work, your life. And that's how you stay relevant in a world that's constantly changing."

Ram nodded thoughtfully. "I think that's what I've been missing—finding time to reflect and apply what I learn."

Rishi smiled, taking another sip of his coffee followed by a deep puff of smoke. "Exactly. Stay curious, stay humble, and remember—every day is an opportunity to learn something new. That's the mindset you need to cultivate, whether you're leading a team, managing a project, or simply navigating life."
They sat quietly for a moment, the sound of the breeze and the distant hum of nature surrounding them.

It was a moment of clarity, one that Priya and Ram knew they would carry forward as they continued their journey—not just in their careers, but in life.

6.1.2 Giving GREAT VIBEs to a thriving team

Rishi started the next session with a ground rule "after establishing trust and credibility, the next critical step for a leader is to create an environment that fosters positivity, motivation, and engagement.

Rishi looked at Ram and Priya thoughtfully before asking, 'Have you ever felt that your words are falling on deaf ears, no matter how logical your arguments are?'

He continued, 'What emotions do you evoke in your team during critical conversations? How do you ensure that your communication resonates with both the hearts and minds of your audience?'

Priya leaned in; her voice tinged with urgency. "Rishi, I agree and I admit. I don't have answers to any of your questions. We've got to get our team back on track. Morale is low, and I can feel the disengagement. What are we missing?"

Rishi, always calm under pressure, studied them for a moment before speaking. "Before we dive into tactics, let me ask you this: Are your team members growing, or do they feel stuck in their roles? Do they feel appreciated for their contributions, or are they just going through the motions?"

Ram frowned, the weight of Rishi's questions sinking in. "I've been so focused on hitting our targets that I haven't really thought about whether they're growing or if they even feel recognized."

Rishi nodded, his expression serious. "That's where the problem begins. It's not just about hitting goals—it's about creating an environment where your team can thrive. When people feel valued, connected, and balanced, they don't just perform—they excel."

Priya looked intrigued, leaning forward. "What exactly are we going to do? How do we create that kind of environment?" Seeing the concern on Ram and Priya's faces, Rishi introduced the next concept. 'To counteract these challenges, it's essential to create an environment that consistently promotes positivity and engagement.

This is where the next method comes into play. Whether it's your team member, client or partner, all of them care for ten elements. Each of these elements plays a crucial role in maintaining a motivated and productive team.

Priya glanced at Ram, then back at Rishi. "Ten elements? Why are these so important? Can't we just focus on getting the job done?"

Rishi shook his head, a hint of a smile on his lips. "That's the trap many leaders fall into. But the method isn't just about getting the job done—it's about how you get it done. When you focus on these elements, you're not just pushing your team to meet goals; you're empowering them to exceed those goals.

It's the difference between a team that's just surviving and one that's truly thriving."

Priya sighed, rubbing her temples. "We've been facing high turnover, low morale, and a lack of innovation. The team feels disconnected, and honestly, so do I. We're all just running on fumes."

Rishi's expression softened, empathy in his eyes. "That's a tough spot to be in, but it's not uncommon. The key is to recognize that the issue isn't just about the work—it's about the environment you've created. When people feel undervalued, overworked, and disconnected from both their leader and the organization's goals, that's when you see high turnover and low morale.

You're not just managing tasks; you're managing people's well-being, their growth, and their sense of purpose." He continued "Many leaders struggle to maintain team morale, especially during periods of high stress or significant change.
"

Ram, his voice full of curiosity, asked, "So how do we turn this around? What do we focus on first?"

Rishi then explained each component in detail:

- **Growth and Development:** Team members are more engaged when they see opportunities for personal and professional growth. Offering paths for advancement, skill development, and continuous learning can drive long-term engagement and satisfaction.
- **Recognition and Appreciation:** Acknowledging and appreciating employees' contributions fosters

motivation and loyalty. Recognition can be formal (e.g., awards) or informal (e.g., verbal praise).

- **Emotional Connection:** Building emotional connections with employees and customers creates strong bonds and loyalty. Emotional engagement goes beyond rational satisfaction and taps into feelings and values.

- **Autonomy and Flexibility:** Autonomy refers to giving employees control over their work, while flexibility involves adapting work conditions to suit individual needs. Both are crucial for engagement, especially in a modern work environment.

- **Trust and Safety:** Trust and psychological safety are fundamental to a productive and innovative work environment. Employees need to feel safe to express ideas, take risks, and be themselves without fear of negative consequences.

- **Values and Purpose:** People are more engaged when they feel their work aligns with their personal values and contributes to a greater purpose. This connection can drive motivation and commitment.

- **Innovation and Creativity**: Encouraging creativity and innovation keeps employees engaged by allowing them to explore new ideas and solutions. It also drives organizational growth and adaptability.
- **Belonging and Community**: A sense of belonging and community strengthens engagement by

making employees feel connected and valued as part of the group. This is crucial for fostering loyalty and teamwork.

- **Equilibrium**: Maintaining a healthy work-life balance is essential for sustained engagement and well-being. Overwork can lead to burnout and disengagement, while balance supports long-term productivity and satisfaction.

This time, Priya preempted Rishi's words. "I get it. We need to give **GREAT VIBEs**!" she exclaimed in ecstasy.

"Correct!" Rishi responded with a smile and a thumbs-up gesture.

'But most of these are the responsibilities of our HR team! ' Ram exclaimed in a confused state.

"Not completely," Rishi corrected Ram. "As a function manager, you are equally or more responsible for the well-being of your team.

HR might occasionally take up some initiatives to boost the morale, but they will never be able to understand the internal team dynamics."

Ram and Priya nodded in agreement.

Rishi smiled, knowing they were ready to listen. "You start by focusing on Growth and Development. People need to feel like they're growing like they're moving forward in their careers.

Offer them opportunities to learn, to expand their skills, and to see a future within the organization. When they grow, they're more engaged."

Priya nodded, a spark of hope in her eyes. "That makes sense. What about Recognition and Appreciation? I've always thought doing your job well should be reward enough."

"Recognition isn't just about rewards," Rishi explained, his tone patient. "It's about acknowledging effort, celebrating successes, and making people feel valued.

When you recognize and appreciate your team, you're telling them that their work matters—that they matter."

Ram leaned back, considering this. "And Emotional Connection? How do we build that when there's so much pressure to perform?"

Rishi's gaze softened, his voice lowering as if sharing a secret. "Emotional Connection is about more than just knowing your team's names. It's about understanding their fears, their motivations, and what drives them. It's about showing that you care—not just about the work, but about them as people.

When you connect on that level, you build trust, and with trust, you can achieve anything."

Priya, feeling more confident, asked, "What about Autonomy and Flexibility? We've been pretty strict about how things get done, but maybe that's part of the problem."

"Absolutely," Rishi agreed, his tone encouraging. "Autonomy and Flexibility allow your team to take ownership of their work. It's about trusting them to make decisions and manage their time.

When people feel trusted, they're more committed. And flexibility—whether it's about work hours or how tasks are completed—shows that you respect their need for balance."

Ram, now fully engaged, said, "And Trust and Safety? How do we ensure our team feels safe enough to speak up and share ideas?"

"Creating a psychologically safe environment is crucial," Rishi replied, his voice firm. People need to know that they can speak their minds without fear of judgment or retribution. Trust is built when you're approachable, supportive, and nonjudgmental. When your team feels safe, they're more likely to innovate, take risks, and contribute their best ideas."

Rishi paused, letting the information sink in. Then, he shared an example to illustrate his point.

Imagine you have a team struggling with low morale and high turnover. As a leader, you recognize the importance of GREAT VIBE and decide to act.

You start by implementing regular check-ins to discuss career goals and development opportunities with each team member.

You introduce a 'Thank You' board where team members can publicly acknowledge each other's efforts.

You organize informal coffee chats to get to know them personally and offer flexible working hours to accommodate their commitments.

You hold regular meetings where team members are encouraged to share their ideas and concerns without fear.

You clearly articulate the organization's values and how each person's work contributes to these goals.

You launch a monthly innovation challenge where the best ideas are recognized and rewarded.

You arrange team-building activities and encourage cross-departmental collaboration.

And finally, you encourage your team to take time off when needed and ensure that workloads are manageable."

Priya and Ram listened intently, imagining how these changes could transform their team.

"But what if we get it wrong?" Priya asked, her voice tinged with concern. "What if we try to apply these principles but end up making things worse?"

Rishi nodded, acknowledging the risk. "Misapplication is a real danger."

He added, 'Neglecting any of the components can also lead to an imbalance that undermines the overall effectiveness of the approach.

For example, promoting balance without providing the necessary support can leave the team feeling overwhelmed and unsupported.'

"If you neglect Growth and Development, your team might feel stagnant and disengaged. Token Recognition can feel disingenuous, reducing its impact.

Focusing too much on Emotional Connection without maintaining professional boundaries can lead to confusion. Too much Autonomy without clear expectations can cause chaos, while excessive Flexibility can lead to a lack of accountability.

Ignoring the need for psychological safety can suppress innovation, and if your team doesn't see the connection between their work and the organization's values, they may feel disconnected.

Stifling Innovation can prevent growth and neglecting the need for Belonging and Community can lead to isolation. Lastly, if you don't prioritize Work-Life Balance, you risk burning out your team."

'There are some more slippery areas'. Rishi added, 'For instance, if you only express gratitude occasionally or only recognize achievements when it's convenient, the team may start to doubt your sincerity.'

Similarly, doing this with one or more team members can send a signal that you are playing favourites.

Ram leaned forward; his curiosity piqued. "Can you give us some practical scenarios where we could apply GREAT VIBE?"

Rishi smiled, pleased to see their enthusiasm. "Of course. Imagine you have a team that's become stagnant, with little growth or innovation.

You apply GREAT VIBE by identifying new learning opportunities, recognizing small wins, and strengthening relationships through team-building exercises.

You allow the team more autonomy in decision-making, ensure a safe space for brainstorming, and re-align their efforts with the organization's mission.

You encourage creative thinking, promote a sense of community, and set clear expectations for work hours while respecting personal time."

Priya's eyes lit up as she imagined the possibilities. "And what if we're building a high-performing team from scratch?" Rishi nodded, his voice filled with conviction. "Then you'd start by assessing each team member's development needs and setting up a mentorship program.

You'd establish regular recognition moments during team meetings, build emotional connections by understanding each team member's motivations, and offer flexible work arrangements.
You'd create an open-door policy for sharing concerns, communicate the organization's values clearly, and foster a culture of innovation by encouraging experimentation.

You'd develop a strong sense of community through social events and collaborative projects, and promote work-life balance by encouraging the use of vacation days and respecting boundaries."

Rishi could sense that Ram and Priya were ready to delve into deeper, more structured approaches to their leadership journey.

Rishi then transitioned to the next framework. 'Now that we've covered how to create a positive and engaging environment with GREAT VIBES, it's time to focus on ensuring clarity in your communication and decision-making.

This is where the next framework comes into play, guiding you to lead your team with precision and purpose.'

6.1.3. Navigating a CLEAR PATH of communication

Ram, eager to move forward, asked, 'Rishi, now that we know how to keep our team engaged, how do we ensure our communication is always clear and effective?'

Priya nodded in agreement, adding, 'Sometimes, despite our best efforts, messages get lost in translation. How can we make sure that our instructions are understood and executed properly?'

Rishi acknowledged their concerns, explaining that miscommunication can lead to misunderstandings, errors, and inefficiencies even in a positive and motivated environment. 'Clear communication is the backbone of effective leadership,' he said, 'It ensures that everyone is aligned and working towards common goals. Without clarity, even the most motivated team can falter.'

To illustrate the point, Rishi described a scenario from his own experience. 'Imagine a project where the stakes were high, and the deadlines were tight.

The leader of this project, confident in their ability to communicate effectively, gave instructions to the team, expecting everything to proceed smoothly.

However, the instructions were vague, and key details were left out. Team members were left guessing about the priorities, and as they tried to interpret the leader's intent, confusion spread like wildfire.'

He continued, 'The design team assumed the primary focus was on aesthetics, while the development team prioritized functionality.

The marketing team, not fully briefed, started promoting features that were not even finalized. In the end, the project fell behind schedule, and the final product was a mishmash of conflicting priorities.

Deadlines were missed, and frustration grew on all sides. The leader, unaware of the confusion they had caused, was baffled by the outcome.

They didn't realize that their communication lacked the clarity needed to ensure everyone was on the same page, leading to a complete breakdown in execution.'

After explaining the pitfalls of unclear communication, Rishi got ready to introduce the next framework: Structured approach to communication

The room was quiet, except for the soft rustling of leaves outside and the distant calls of birds echoing through the trees.

Priya and Ram sat across from Rishi, their minds still buzzing with the concepts of GREAT VIBE.

But they knew there was more to learn—more tools they needed to master if they were to truly turn things around. They also reflected on the last example Rishi gave about a communication issue.

Priya broke the silence, her voice steady but curious. "Rishi, we've talked about creating the right environment with GREAT VIBE, but what about our communication?

We've had moments where things got lost in translation, and it's cost us. How do we make sure we're communicating effectively?"

Rishi nodded, seeing that they were ready for the next lesson. "Communication is key to everything we've discussed. If you can't communicate clearly and effectively, even the best ideas can fall flat. That's where the next framework comes in. It's designed to guide you through every conversation, ensuring that you're not just talking, but truly connecting."

Rishi leaned forward, his eyes locking onto Priya and Ram. "Let me ask you this—when you're in a conversation,

- How often do you find yourself thinking about your response rather than really listening to the other person?

- Do you ever walk away from a discussion feeling like you weren't fully understood, or worse, that you misunderstood the other person?"

Ram frowned, recognizing the truth in Rishi's words. "More often than I'd like to admit. It's easy to get caught up in what I want to say next, especially when I'm under pressure."

"And that's where the problem begins," Rishi said, his tone serious. "The next framework is about more than just talking—it's about truly engaging with the other person, understanding their perspective, and ensuring that your communication is clear, thoughtful, and impactful."

Priya looked intrigued, leaning in. "So, what exactly is that? How does it help us navigate these conversations?"

Rishi smiled, pleased with their interest. He explained the components of the framework.

- **Concentrate:** Focus your attention fully on the speaker and the expected outcome.
- **Listen:** Actively listen to what is being said without interruptions or assumptions.
- **Empathize:** Put yourself in the other person's shoes to truly understand their emotions and perspective.
- **Analyze:** Analyse the information presented and evaluate the context, emotions, and facts.
- **Reflect:** Pause and reflect on the information. Ensure your response is measured, thoughtful, contextual and covers all implications.
- **Paraphrase:** Paraphrase or restate key points to ensure understanding and clarification.

- **Articulate:** Express your response, clearly, assertively and thoughtfully.
- **Tune up:** Fine-tune your message, adjusting it for clarity, tone, and audience impact.

- **Harmonize**: Strive for mutual understanding and alignment, ensuring that both parties are on the same page.

"In summary, the framework stands for Concentrate, Listen, Empathize, Analyze, Reflect, Paraphrase, Articulate, tune up, and Harmonize.

In short, **CLEAR PATH**.

It's a step-by-step approach that guides you through the process of communication, from focusing your attention fully on the speaker to ensuring that both parties walk away with a clear and mutual understanding."

Ram nodded, seeing the potential. "So, it's about being present in the conversation, not just waiting for our turn to speak."

"Exactly," Rishi confirmed. "When you follow the CLEAR PATH, you're not just communicating—you're connecting. And that connection is what drives effective teamwork and leadership."

Priya sighed, rubbing her temples as she recalled recent miscommunications. "We've had issues where we thought we were clear, but the message got twisted somewhere along the way. It's frustrating because it feels like we're saying one thing, but the team is hearing something else."

Rishi nodded, understanding their frustration. "That's a common challenge, and it usually happens when we're not fully engaged in the communication process.

We think we're being clear, but if we're not truly concentrating, listening, or empathizing, the message can get lost or misinterpreted."

However, this is a very fundamental hygiene of any communication, and this is one thing that can make or break every interaction. It's also the step many people take for granted.

 "But not just any kind of listening—active listening. It's the ability to really tune in, to focus fully on the other person, and to understand not just what they're saying but why they're saying it. Most people listen to respond, not to understand."

Rishi and Priya nodded in full agreement.
Let's take a moment to understand various types of listening, each suited to different situations. Mastering these types can change how you interact with others."

Rishi showed a slide on Active listening.

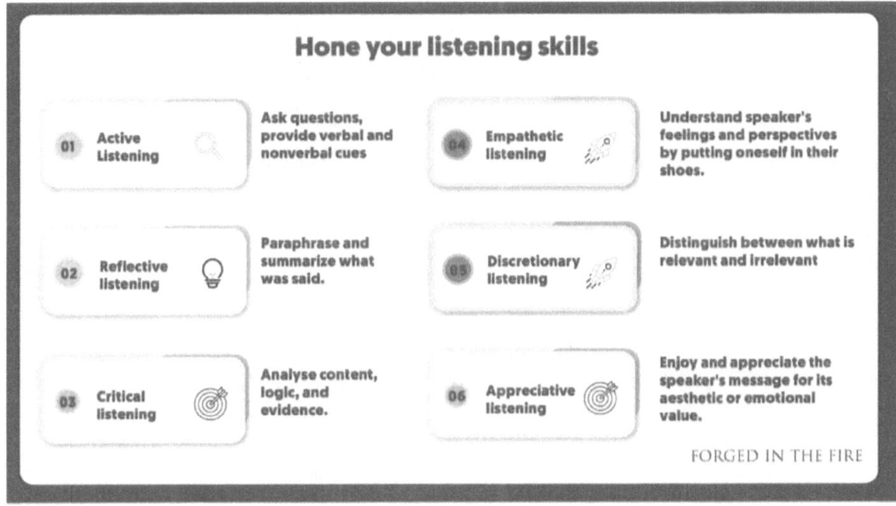

1. Active Listening:

"This is what we often think of first. It's listening with full attention, absorbing what the speaker is saying, and responding thoughtfully. Your focus is entirely on the speaker—no distractions, no interruptions."

2. Reflective Listening:

"Here, you reflect back what the other person is saying, almost like a mirror. It helps to confirm understanding. You can say something like, 'So, what I'm hearing is…' This ensures you're on the same page."

3. Critical Listening:

"This involves analyzing and evaluating the content. It's not just about listening for the sake of it—you're actively assessing the message for accuracy and logic. You'll often use this when evaluating information, like in meetings or decision-making processes."

4. Empathetic Listening:

"Sometimes, people don't want advice or analysis—they just want to be heard and understood. Empathetic listening involves putting yourself in the speaker's shoes, trying to understand their feelings and perspective."

5. Discretionary Listening:

"This one's more nuanced. Discretionary listening is knowing when to listen and when to disengage. Sometimes, not everything said is important or relevant. It's about discerning what's worth paying attention to."

6. Appreciative Listening:

"And then there's listening for enjoyment. Appreciative listening is what we do when we listen to music, attend a lecture, or hear someone speak on a topic we admire. It's about savoring the experience."

Rishi showed another slide that has a table to clarify which type of listening to use in different situations:

Listening types

#	Situation	Type of Listening	Objective
1	Team Meetings/Decision Making	Critical Listening	To assess the information and evaluate options.
2	1-on-1 Conversations with Team	Active/Empathetic Listening	To fully understand and connect emotionally.
3	Giving Feedback to a Colleague	Reflective Listening	To ensure mutual understanding and clarity.
4	Casual Conversations/Personal Growth	Appreciative Listening	To enjoy and appreciate the exchange.
5	Handling a Complaint	Empathetic Listening	To acknowledge the speaker's feelings fully.
6	Time-Sensitive Conversations	Discretionary Listening	To prioritize what's important.

FORGED IN THE FIRE

Priya and Ram studied the table, nodding as Rishi explained each scenario.

"Listening is important," Rishi continued, "but you must also diagnose the situation like a doctor. I want to introduce you to a method medical professionals use to diagnose patients called SOAP, developed by Dr. Larry Weed."

Ram raised an eyebrow. "SOAP? Interesting"

Rishi smiled and moved to the next slide.

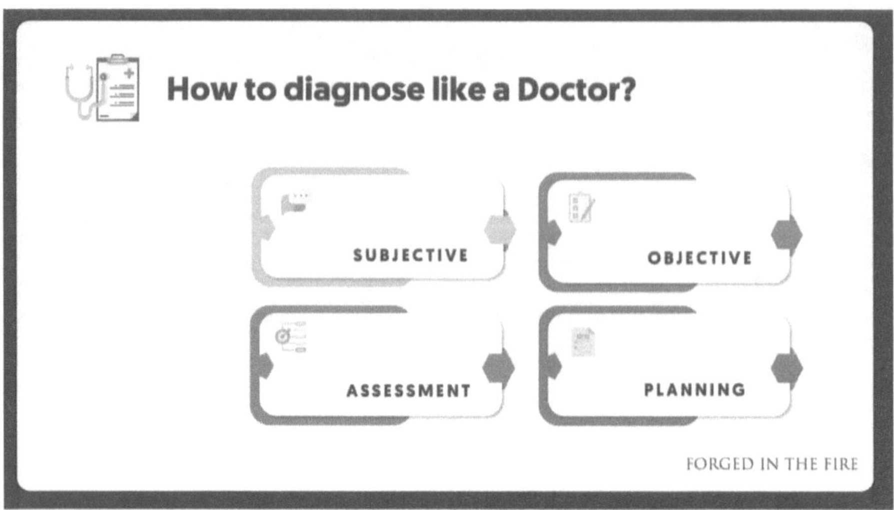

Subjective

"This is what the speaker or 'patient' is telling you in their own words. In a work context, this might be when a team member explains a problem they're facing or a challenge they're encountering."

Objective

"This is what you can observe or measure. It's the facts. If a team member is consistently missing deadlines, the objective part is the missed deadlines, not just their explanation."

Assessment

"This is where you combine the subjective and objective information to form a diagnosis. It's about interpreting the situation based on what you've heard and seen."

Plan

"Finally, you create a plan of action. Like a doctor would prescribe treatment, you need to develop a solution, or next steps based on your assessment."

Rishi stepped back, looking at Priya and Ram to gauge their reactions.

"When you listen like a doctor, you're not just passively receiving information—you're diagnosing the situation. The SOAP framework helps you structure your thinking, and when combined with the right type of listening, it allows you to respond thoughtfully and effectively."

Priya, clearly impressed, asked, "So when we're diagnosing a team issue or a conflict, we can use SOAP to guide the conversation?"

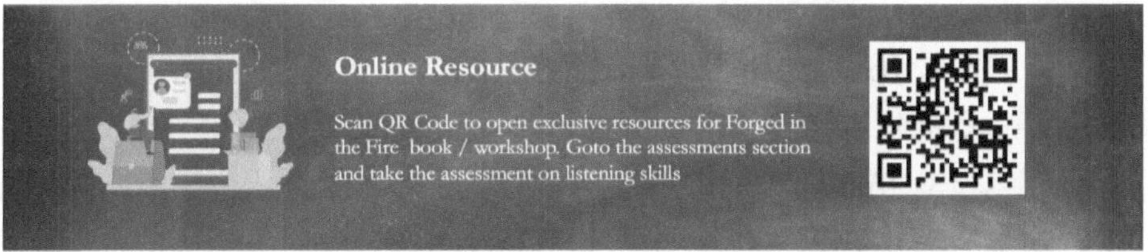

"Exactly," Rishi said. "By starting with what the other person says (Subjective), you can then compare it to what you know or observe (Objective).

From there, you assess the real issue and then create a plan to move forward."

Ram's eyes lit up. "This makes so much sense. It's like we're diagnosing the root cause, not just addressing the symptoms."

Rishi nodded. "That's the key. Listening is powerful when it's structured and purposeful.

You'll find that using the correct type of listening in the proper context, combined with SOAP, will drastically improve how you handle conversations, conflicts, and even negotiations."

Rishi paused, looking at both Priya and Ram. "The biggest mistake most people make is thinking listening is passive. It's not.

Listening is active, intentional, and strategic. You need to:

- **Stay focused:** Eliminate distractions and give the speaker your full attention.
- **Listen without judgment:** Don't rush to conclusions or let your biases cloud your perception.
- **Use reflective techniques:** Paraphrase and reflect to ensure mutual understanding.

- **Apply empathy:** Try to understand not just the words, but the feelings behind them.
- **Be patient:** Don't rush to fill the silence—let the other person express themselves fully.

When you approach listening this way, you'll uncover insights that most people miss. And that can make all the difference in leadership, teamwork, and communication."

Priya and Ram both nodded, the gravity of the lesson settling in. They knew this wasn't just about becoming better listeners—it was about becoming more effective leaders and more empathetic individuals.

Rishi added "The leader has to practice active listening and push everyone in the team to cultivate the habit."

Both nodded in full agreement.

Eager to learn, Ram asked, "So how do we use CLEAR PATH to ensure that doesn't happen?"

Rishi leaned back in his chair, his voice calm but firm. "It starts with Concentration. Focus your attention fully on the speaker and the expected outcome. When you're distracted or thinking ahead, you miss important details."

"Then you Listen," Rishi continued, "Actively listen to what is being said without interruptions or assumptions. Too often, we listen to respond rather than to understand. But if you're listening, you're absorbing the message fully."

"Empathize," he said, his tone softening. "Put yourself in the other person's shoes to truly understand their emotions and perspective. This isn't just about hearing their words—it's about feeling what they're feeling."

Priya nodded; her interest piqued. "So, it's not just about the facts—the emotions behind them."

"Exactly," Rishi replied. "Next, you Analyze. Evaluate the information presented—consider the context, the emotions, and the facts. Don't just take things at face value—think critically about what's being said."

"And then Reflect," Rishi continued. "Pause and reflect on the information. Ensure your response is measured, thoughtful, and contextual. It's about taking a moment to process before you react."

Ram, feeling more confident, asked, "What about Paraphrase? How does that help?"

"Paraphrasing is crucial," Rishi explained. "It's about restating key points to ensure understanding and clarification. When you paraphrase, you're checking that you've understood the message correctly—and that the other person feels understood."

"Then comes Articulate," Rishi said, his voice steady. "Express your response clearly, assertively, and thoughtfully. It's not just about what you say, but how you say it. Your tone, your choice of words—they all matter."

"Tune-up," Rishi continued, "is about fine-tuning your message, adjusting it for clarity, tone, and audience impact. It's about making sure your message is clear and resonates with the listener."

"And finally," Rishi said, leaning in, "Harmonize. Strive for mutual understanding and alignment, ensuring that both parties are on the same page. It's not enough to speak your mind—you must ensure your message has been received and understood as you intended."

Rishi paused, allowing the information to sink in. Then, he shared an example to illustrate the framework in action.

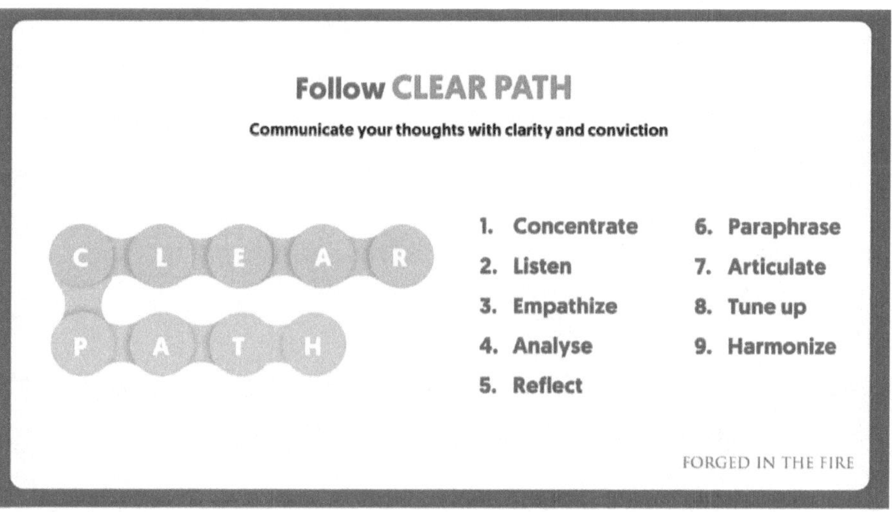

Imagine you're in a meeting with a team member who's frustrated because they feel their ideas aren't being heard.

You start by **Concentrating**—putting aside your thoughts and focusing entirely on them.

As they speak, you **Listen** actively, not interrupting or assuming. You notice their tone and body language, so you **Empathize**, understanding that their frustration is as much about feeling undervalued as it is about the idea itself.

You then **Analyze** the situation, considering not just their words but the context—maybe they've been overlooked in the past.

Before responding, you **Reflect**, making sure your reply is thoughtful.

You **Paraphrase** their concerns to ensure you've understood them correctly—'So, I'm hearing that you feel your contributions aren't being recognized, is that right?'

Then, you **Articulate** your response clearly, acknowledging their feelings and offering a solution.

You **Tune** up your message, ensuring it's respectful and constructive.

Finally, you **Harmonize** by checking in—'Does that address your concerns? Are we aligned on the way forward?'

By following the CLEAR PATH, you resolve the issue and strengthen your relationship with the team member."

Priya, ever the realist, asked, "But what if we mess this up? What are the risks if we don't apply CLEAR PATH correctly?"

Rishi's expression grew serious. "Misapplication can lead to several issues. If you're not fully Concentrating, you might miss key details.

Failing to Listen actively can result in misunderstandings. If you don't Empathize, the other person might feel unheard or undervalued. Poor Analysis can lead to misjudgments, and you might react impulsively if you don't Reflect.

Neglecting to Paraphrase can cause miscommunication, and if you don't Articulate clearly, your message might be confusing.

If you don't Tune up your message, it might not resonate with your audience, and failing to Harmonize can leave both parties with lingering doubts or unresolved issues."

Ram leaned forward, intrigued. "Can you give us some scenarios where we might need to use CLEAR PATH?"
Rishi smiled, pleased with their engagement. "Of course. Imagine you're negotiating a deal with a client who's unhappy with your terms. You start by Concentrating fully on their concerns, Listening without interrupting.

You Empathize with their position, recognizing that they're under pressure too. You Analyze their objections, considering both the facts and their emotional state.

Before responding, you Reflect, ensuring your reply is measured.

You Paraphrase their concerns to confirm you've understood them correctly.

Then, you Articulate a revised offer, adjusting your message to ensure it's clear and persuasive.

You tune up your tone to ensure its conciliatory and not confrontational.

Finally, you Harmonize by confirming that the new terms are acceptable and that you're both aligned moving forward."

Priya's eyes lit up as she imagined applying the framework. "And what if we're dealing with a team conflict?"

"In that case," Rishi explained, "you'd use CLEAR PATH to navigate the conversation carefully.

You'd Concentrate fully on each person's perspective, listen without taking sides, and Empathize with both parties.

You'd Analyze the underlying issues, reflect before responding to avoid escalating the conflict.

Paraphrase to ensure you've captured their concerns accurately.

Articulate a fair resolution, Tune up your message to maintain a calm and neutral tone, and Harmonize by ensuring both parties feel heard and agree on the way forward."

As Rishi finished, Priya and Ram felt a new sense of clarity. They realized that by mastering the CLEAR PATH framework, they could transform not just their conversations but their entire approach to leadership.

6.2. Being organized and ready

6.2.1 Prioritising activities

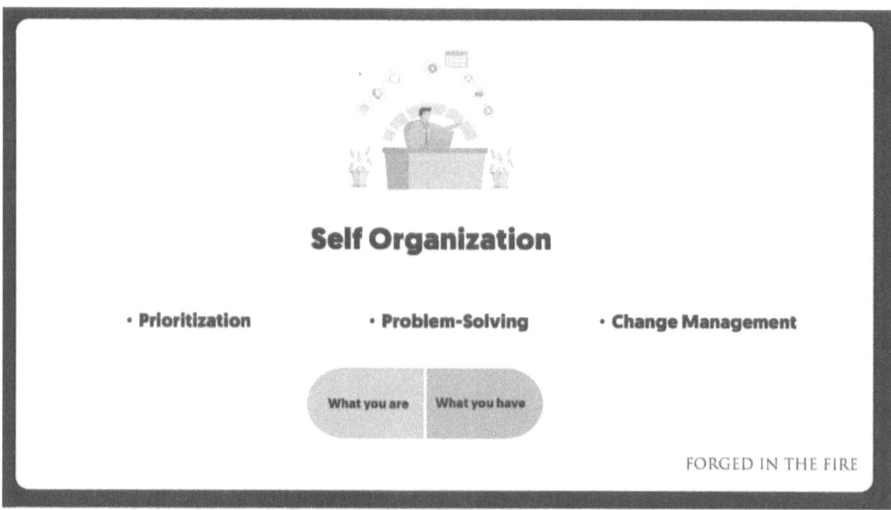

The late afternoon sun streamed through the office windows, casting long shadows on the floor. Priya and Ram were deep in thought, processing the wealth of information they had absorbed so far. But they knew there was more to learn—especially when it came to organizing their work and managing change.

Priya broke the silence, her voice steady but laced with a hint of frustration. "Rishi, we've been juggling so many tasks lately. It feels like we're constantly busy but not necessarily productive.

How do we figure out what really matters?"
Rishi, ever the calm presence in the storm, smiled slightly.

 "You're not alone in feeling that way, Priya.

The key to cutting through the noise is learning how to prioritize effectively.

That's where the PRIORITIZE framework comes in. It's all about focusing on what truly matters and managing your time and tasks efficiently."

Rishi leaned forward, his eyes serious as he posed his questions. "How often do you find yourselves overwhelmed by the sheer number of tasks on your plate? Do you ever end the day feeling like you were busy but didn't actually accomplish anything significant?"

Ram sighed, nodding in agreement. "Too often. There are days when I'm constantly working, but by the end, it feels like I didn't make any real progress."

"And that's a common struggle," Rishi said, understanding their frustration. "That's why it's essential to prioritize.

Without a clear plan, it's easy to get lost in the chaos of daily demands. But when you prioritize effectively, you can focus on what's most important and ensure that you're making meaningful progress."

Priya, curious as ever, asked, "So how do we start? What's the first step in prioritizing?"

Rishi smiled, pleased with her eagerness to learn. "PRIORITIZE stands for

- **Pinpoint** Your Objectives
- **Rank** Tasks by Urgency and Importance
- **Identify** Key Deadlines
- **Organize** Tasks into Manageable Chunks
- **Review** and Adjust Regularly
- **Implement** Time Management Techniques
- **Tackle** the Most Critical Tasks First
- **Include** Time for Long-Term Goals
- **Zero** In on Bottlenecks
- **Evaluate** Outcomes

It's a comprehensive approach to organizing your work so that you're not just busy—you're productive."

Ram rubbed his temples, recalling recent days filled with back-to-back meetings and never-ending to-do lists.

"We've been so caught up in the day-to-day that it feels like we're constantly putting out fires. How do we ensure we're working toward our long-term goals?"

Rishi nodded, recognizing the challenge. "That's a common issue when you're managing a lot of responsibilities.

The key is to start by clearly identifying your key objectives— what are you working toward, and why is it important?

Once you have that clarity, you can start ranking your tasks by urgency and importance, ensuring that you focus on what truly matters."

Priya leaned in, eager for practical advice. "So, how do we go about prioritizing our tasks?"

"Start by pinpointing your objectives," Rishi advised, his tone firm. "Understand what you're working toward and why it's important.

Once you have a clear goal in mind, you can begin to rank your tasks by urgency and importance. N

ot all tasks are created equal—some will have a more significant impact on your objectives than others."

"Then, identify key deadlines," Rishi continued.

"Map out the critical deadlines for each task. This will help you organize your tasks into manageable chunks, breaking down larger projects into smaller, actionable steps."

Priya nodded, jotting down notes. "That makes sense. But what if new tasks or information come up?"

"That's where reviewing and adjusting regularly comes in," Rishi explained. "You need to be flexible and willing to adjust your priorities as new tasks or information arise.

It's not about sticking rigidly to a plan but about being adaptable."

Ram, feeling more confident, asked, "What about time management? I've heard about techniques like time blocking, but I'm not sure how to implement them effectively."

Rishi smiled, pleased with the direction of the conversation.

"Implementing time management techniques like time blocking, the Pomodoro Technique, or batching similar tasks can help you stay focused and productive. It's about making the most of your time and ensuring that you're tackling the most critical tasks first."

"And don't forget to include time for long-term goals," Rishi added. "It's easy to get caught up in immediate tasks, but it's crucial to make time for your strategic goals as well."

Priya, now fully engaged, asked, "What if we hit a bottleneck? How do we handle obstacles that slow us down?"

"Zero in on bottlenecks," Rishi advised, his tone serious. "Identify and address any obstacles that are slowing down your progress.

Once you've completed your tasks, evaluate the outcomes. This will help you learn what worked well and what could be improved, allowing you to refine your approach moving forward."

Rishi paused, letting the information sink in before sharing a practical example.

"Imagine you're leading a project with tight deadlines and multiple deliverables. You start by pinpointing your objectives—identifying what the project's ultimate goal is.

Next, you rank the tasks by urgency and importance, recognizing that some deliverables are critical to the project's success, while others are secondary.

You map out key deadlines, breaking down the project into manageable chunks with clear milestones. As the project progresses, you regularly review and adjust your priorities, accommodating any changes or new information.

You implement time management techniques, such as time blocking, to stay focused and tackle the most critical tasks first each day.

You ensure that your schedule includes time for immediate tasks and long-term strategic goals.

When you encounter a bottleneck, you zero in on it, addressing the issue head-on.

Finally, once the project is complete, you evaluate the outcomes, identifying areas for improvement in your process."

Ram and Priya listened intently, picturing how to apply this to their work.

Ram leaned forward, eager for more practical advice. "Can you give us some scenarios where we might need to use PRIORITIZE?"

Rishi smiled, pleased with their engagement. "Of course. Imagine you're managing a major project with multiple moving parts.

You use PRIORITIZE to pinpoint your objectives, rank tasks by urgency and importance, and identify critical deadlines.

You review and adjust your priorities as new information comes in, ensuring you're always focused on what matters most.

You implement time management techniques to stay productive, tackling the most critical tasks first each day.

You make time for long-term goals, addressing any bottlenecks as they arise. Once the project is complete, you evaluate the outcomes, learning from what worked and what didn't."

Priya's eyes lit up as she imagined applying the framework. "And what if we're dealing with a rapidly changing situation?" "In that case," Rishi explained, "you'd need to manage CHANGE effectively.

It's about being proactive and adaptable, communicating clearly, and handling resistance with empathy.

You align the change with your vision, guide your team through the transition, and keep them engaged and motivated throughout the process.

After implementing the change, you evaluate its effectiveness and gather feedback to ensure continuous improvement."

To sum up

- Pinpoint Your Objectives
- Rank Tasks by Urgency and Importance
- Identify Key Deadlines
- Organize Tasks into Manageable Chunks
- Review and Adjust Regularly
- Implement Time Management Techniques
- Tackle the Most Critical Tasks
- Include Time for Long-Term Goals
- Zero In on Bottlenecks
- Evaluate Outcomes

6.2.2 CHANGE for the better

It was the afternoon of their second-to-last day. Priya and Ram looked tense as they started realizing the sheer magnitude of the upcoming project. Rishi, noticing their concern, leaned forward, smiling softly.

"I can see you're both thinking about the challenges you'll face," Rishi said, his voice calm but knowing. "Change is never easy, is it?"

Ram let out a sigh and leaned back in his chair. "Yeah, it's not just the client. We're introducing new AI tools and changing workflows. The team's going to resist this. People don't like change, especially not this much at all."

Priya nodded in agreement. "It's not just the technical changes either—it's a whole mindset shift. How do we get everyone on board with this?"

Rishi stood and walked over to the whiteboard, picking up a marker. He wrote the letters "C-H-A-N-G-E" in bold strokes.

"That's exactly what I wanted to talk about. This, my friends, is the CHANGE framework. It's designed to help you navigate resistance and smoothly lead your team through transitions."

- Communicate Clearly
- Handle Resistance
- Align with Vision
- Navigate the Transition
- Generate Engagement:
- Evaluate and Evolve

Ram and Priya leaned in, intrigued. "Alright, how does it work?" Ram asked.

Rishi pointed at the first letter. "The first step is Communicate Clearly. When people don't understand why change is happening, they fear it.

It would help if you were transparent about the reasons for the change—what's at stake, how it benefits the company, and, significantly, how it affects them personally.

Fear thrives in the unknown. By communicating openly, you eliminate most of that anxiety."

Priya nodded earnestly. "So, we need to explain the why behind the change, not just the what."

"Exactly," Rishi continued. "And it's crucial that you listen to their concerns too.

Use the CLEAR PATH framework we discussed earlier.

This leads to the next step: Handle Resistance. Resistance will happen—people are wired to resist change. But don't fight it head-on.

Instead, try to understand where it's coming from.

Is it fear of losing control? A lack of skills? Or simply the comfort of the status quo?

Once you understand the root of their resistance, you can address it."

"So, instead of forcing the change, we bring them into the process?" Priya asked, her brow furrowing slightly.

"Exactly," Rishi said, nodding. "People resist what they feel is imposed on them, but they'll support what they feel they own.

That's where you move to the next step—Align with Vision. Every change needs to be tied to a larger vision. You need to help your team see how this change fits into the bigger picture—how it benefits the company and creates new opportunities for them personally."

Ram looked thoughtful. "So, it's not just about making the change—it's about showing them that it's part of something bigger."

"Yes," Rishi agreed. "People need to see that the disruption is leading to growth, not just chaos.

The next step is Navigate the Transition. Change doesn't happen overnight. You need a clear plan with milestones and support systems along the way. It's not just about implementing the change, but making sure your team knows the path forward and that you're there to guide them."

Priya jotted down notes as she listened. "So, we break the change into smaller, achievable steps, and celebrate progress as we go?"

"Exactly," Rishi said. "If you try to do everything at once, people will freeze. It needs to feel manageable. Then, there's Generate Engagement.

You can't just make the change and expect people to stay on board. You need to constantly check in, ask for feedback, and keep them involved in the process.

Engagement is what keeps people motivated through difficult transitions."
Ram smiled, feeling a sense of clarity. "So, it's not a one-time thing. We have to keep them engaged and feeling like part of the solution."

"Exactly," Rishi said again, pleased with their understanding. "And finally, Evaluate and Evolve.

Once the change is implemented, it's essential to assess how it went. What worked? What didn't? And what can be done better next time? Change is dynamic—you'll always be learning and refining."

Ram and Priya exchanged glances, the weight of their initial anxiety lifting. "This makes a lot of sense," Priya said. "It's not just about making a change—it's about guiding people through it."

"Exactly," Rishi said, his tone reassuring. "If you communicate clearly, address resistance, and show them the bigger picture, the change becomes less of an obstacle and more of an opportunity. Trust me, the CHANGE framework will help you lead your team through this transition."

Priya smiled, feeling more confident than before. "Thanks, Rishi. I think we can handle this."

Rishi gave a knowing smile. "I know you can."

As Rishi finished, Priya and Ram felt a renewed sense of clarity. They realized that by mastering the PRIORITIZE and CHANGE frameworks, they could not only manage their time and tasks more effectively but also lead their team through change with confidence and success.

6.2.3 Mastering the Problem Solving

Rishi leaned forward, his tone focused. "Now that you know how to prioritize and manage change, lets now cover problem solving.

This framework is your go-to for problem-solving. It's designed to help you align your team, separate people from the problem, overcome biases, and execute a solution effectively."

Rishi looked at Priya and Ram, his gaze intent. "

- When a problem arises within your team, do you find it challenging to get everyone on the same page?
- Do interpersonal issues sometimes cloud the real problem?
- And when it comes to finding solutions, do you struggle with biases that might skew your judgment?"

Ram nodded, recognizing the challenges. "It's easy to get caught up in the emotions of a situation, and that can make it hard to focus on the actual problem."

"And that's where SSOLVER comes in," Rishi said. "It helps you navigate these challenges with a structured approach."

Rishi began to explain, his voice steady. "Start with Set the Stage. Align your team by setting clear goals and establishing ground rules for collaboration. This creates a shared understanding and focus."

"Next," he continued, "Separate People from the Problem. Acknowledge and address interpersonal issues separately before focusing on the problem itself. This ensures that emotions don't cloud your judgment."

"Then," Rishi added, "Overcome Biases. Use practical tools and exercises to identify and mitigate cognitive and emotional biases. This allows you to approach the problem with a clear, objective mindset."

Priya leaned in, eager to learn more. "And how do we dive deeper into the problem itself?"

"That's where Learn about the Problem comes in," Rishi explained. "Adopt a learner mindset and use diverse analytical tools to thoroughly understand the problem.

This might involve gathering data, seeking different perspectives, or breaking down the problem into smaller parts."

"And then we move on to Visualize Alternatives," Rishi continued. "Foster creative thinking and explore a wide range of possible solutions. Don't settle for the first idea—encourage your team to think outside the box."

"Next," Rishi said, "Execute the Plan with Change Management. Focus on effective execution, incorporating change management strategies to handle resistance and ensure success. This is where you turn ideas into action."

"Finally," Rishi concluded, "Reflect Thoroughly. Use structured reflection techniques to capture lessons learned and improve future problem-solving efforts. Reflection ensures that you learn from each experience and continue to grow as a leader."

To summarize, apply the SSOLVER framework to address your day-to-day issues.

- Set the Stage and Alignment
- Separate people from the problem
- Overcome biases
- Learn about the problem
- Visualise alternatives and the best possible ways to resolve the issue
- Execute the plan
- Reflect on the issue, side effects, and recurrence

Rishi continued "We will now move to the core communication skills starting from written communication"

Priya and Ram were waiting for this moment. They are desperate to understand how to transform their report for the next client meeting.

6.3 Mastering Written Communication

The room was quiet as evening settled in. Priya and Ram had spent the day absorbing a wealth of new knowledge, but they knew their journey was far from over. As they prepared to dive into the next topic, they couldn't help but feel excitement and anticipation.

Priya broke the silence, her voice thoughtful. "Rishi, we've covered a lot about organizing our work and leading our team, but what about our written communication?

We've struggled to communicate clearly and persuasively, especially in our reports and presentations."
Rishi, always ready with a solution, nodded thoughtfully. "Written communication is critical, especially in a fast-paced business environment. It's not just about what you say but how you say it.

The way you present your ideas can make all the difference in whether they're embraced or ignored. That's why we need to talk about four special frameworks now."

6.3.1 PRESENTing your ideas with ease

Rishi leaned forward, his tone focused. "Let's start with framework for presentations.

This framework is all about crafting your message to persuade and resonate with your audience. It's not enough to just share information—you need to do it in a way that's engaging and compelling."

Rishi looked at Priya and Ram, his gaze intent.

- "When you write a report or prepare a presentation, do you think about who your audience is and what they care about?

- Do you make an effort to engage them from the start, or do you dive straight into the details?"

Ram nodded slowly, realization dawning. "I've always focused on the facts, but I haven't really thought about tailoring the message to the audience.

I just assumed the information would speak for itself."

"And that's where many people go wrong," Rishi replied.

"The PRESENT framework is designed to help you craft a message that informs and persuades. Let me break it down for you."

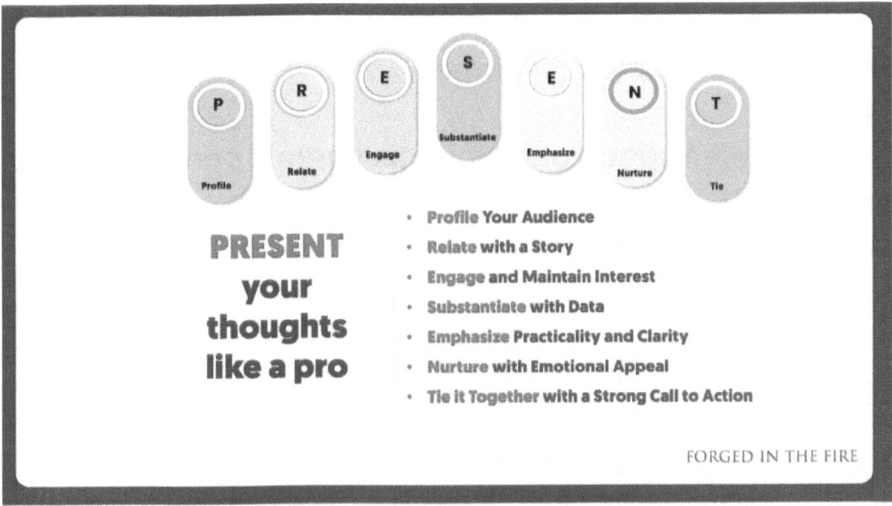

- Profile Your Audience
- Relate with a Story
- Engage and Maintain Interest
- Substantiate with Data
- Emphasize Practicality and Clarity
- Nurture with Emotional Appeal
- Tie it Together with a Strong Call to Action

Rishi began to outline the framework, his voice steady. "First, **Profile Your Audience.** Understand who they are, what they care about, and what they need from you. Tailor your message to their needs and interests."

"Next, **Relate with a Story**," Rishi continued. "Start with a compelling narrative that connects emotionally. People are more likely to remember a story than a list of facts. It helps them relate to the message on a deeper level."

Priya, intrigued, asked, "But what if we're dealing with data? How do we keep them engaged?"

"That's where **Engage and Maintain Interest comes in**," Rishi explained. "Use interactive elements, dynamic delivery, and ask questions to keep your audience involved.

Even when presenting data, make it relatable—show them how it impacts them directly."

"And of course, you need to **Substantiate with Data**," Rishi added. "Back up your points with relevant, impactful data. This gives your message credibility and shows that your arguments are grounded in reality."

Ram leaned in, his interest piqued. "What about making the content clear and actionable?"

"That's where **Emphasize Practicality** and Clarity comes in," Rishi said. "Make your content clear, focused, and actionable. People need to understand exactly what you're saying and what they should do next."

"Finally," Rishi concluded, "**Nurture with Emotional Appeal** and Tie it Together with a Strong Call to Action. Use emotional content to deepen the connection and persuasion, and end with a clear, compelling directive. This is how you guide your audience to the outcome you want."

Rishi paused briefly and continued.

When it comes to presentations, 'Content is the king and Context is the Kingpin.'

Let's assume you want to create a presentation for a prospect. So, it is important to consider the intent and the objective of the presentation before we plunge into the creation of the slides.

We need to answer the following questions before creating every presentation.

- What are the stakes?
- What is the delegate/participant profile?
- What is the path that they are most likely to take?
- What is the path that we want them to take?
- Are we on the same page with them?
- Do we have that AAA (Triple A) rated person in the group?
- What are questions that we need to ask them?
- What do we expect from them towards the end of the journey?

Profiling stage is the most appropriate time to have a brainstorming with all the stakeholders and get all of them on the same page.

This is the stage where we plan with the end in mind.

The first step in the journey is to visualize the benefits of the prospect giving the mandate.

It could trigger a press release, a grand gala victory party, etc. This visualization will not only trigger the motivation but will also help every member realize the importance of focusing on the final pitch.

1. What are the stakes?

This is by far the most critical question. This question determines what you will win and are likely to lose, depending on whether the final pitch is successful. The higher the stakes, the greater the number of preparations involving more team members.

In this case, it is a prestigious multi-million-dollar project with a Fortune 500 client. Success would mean an excellent head start for the entire vertical, and failure would mean several heads might roll!

Although there is no scientific basis for what I am saying, you must take at least one hour to prepare each slide.

If you plan to show 30 slides, you need approximately 30 hours of preparation. You may accelerate the development time with several online tools, but always uphold the importance of preparation.

This is irrespective of the readily available content.

2. What is the delegate/participant profile?

We can guess their intent by examining the participants' designations/roles and answering the questions.

Network Strength: Member in our team who knows him/her best from the past.

Knowledge: His/her understanding of the product, service or subject area.

Perception: Past experience with our product or service. Past association with the organization.

The delegate profiling gives us very good insights into the visitors' team profiles and expectations from the meeting.

3. What is the path that they are most likely to take?

This is probably the best time to re-look at the client's problem statement and match what's on it with our delivery items. This should give us the list of reasons why they would want to talk to us.

- What are the top five things that they expect from us? For a business pitch, it is the capability to showcase. For a seminar, it is the subject knowledge or the networking opportunity.

- What are the top five things that appealed to them?
- What is the time frame for the presentation?
- Who are the participants?
- What do they intend to see?

4. What is the path that we want them to take? Are we on the same page with them?

The above questions serve to give us clarity on client expectations. The next step is to match our showcase theme with their expectations.

In case of a mismatch or deviation, it is best to set the expectations right by communicating with the project's primary driver, usually the prospect organization's SPOC (Single Point of Contact).

5 Do we have that AAA (Triple A) rated person in the group?

While making investments, we look for the rating of the stock/bond and will make sure that it has the highest rating, i.e., AAA.

Similarly, we must deal with the person with the AAA (Triple A) rating. The person who has the following attributes is the person:

- Appetite
- Affordability
- Authority

This person may or may not have the need, but if he/she has an appetite for our solution, that is sufficient for making our pitch.

Similarly, if there is affordability and authority, we are talking to the right person.

People who do not qualify for these three aspects cannot decide independently. We can still talk to them because they may be the opinion makers, but the person with the AAA rating is the ultimate.

6. What are the questions that we need to ask them?

Ask more than you tell.

We often assume that we know much about the prospect or the delegate. The answer in most cases is 'No'.

It never hurts to ask for more information. It indicates to the other party that we are serious about our business and interested in their choices and preferences. On the contrary, not asking questions might be perceived as audacity or ignorance.

Every prospect (be it a client or an investor) wants questions to be asked. They don't expect you to have answers to all questions. In fact, they will respect the people who ask the right questions.

The right questions will yield more answers and give you further clues about the expectations. They will also elevate the prospect's ownership/involvement levels.

7. What do we expect from them towards the journey's end?

This is the ultimate question. What do we want? Cheque to be cut immediately? Agreement to be signed? Pledge for more support? Applause?

Rishi concluded the explanation on presentations. After this session, Priya and ram clearly understood their shortcomings and the mistake of over reliance on AI tools.

6.3.2 Weaving a compelling STORY

Priya smiled, feeling a new sense of clarity. "I see how PRESENT can help us craft our message. But you mentioned using stories—how do we do that effectively?"

Rishi's eyes lit up, knowing they were getting to the heart of the matter. "The next framework is about storytelling. Infact this is a component of the present framework. You can also use this standalone while talking in meetings.

Crux of the storytelling about setting the stage, triggering the conflict, outlining the journey, revealing the resolution, and ending with your key takeaway."

Rishi leaned back in his chair, his voice steady.

- "When you're telling a story in your communication, do you make sure to set the scene first?
- Do you introduce a central conflict that grabs attention, and do you take your audience through the journey before revealing the resolution?"

Ram frowned slightly, considering the question. "I usually just focus on the facts, but I'm starting to see how a story could make the message more impactful."

"And you're right," Rishi agreed. "A well-told story can transform your communication. Let's break it down."

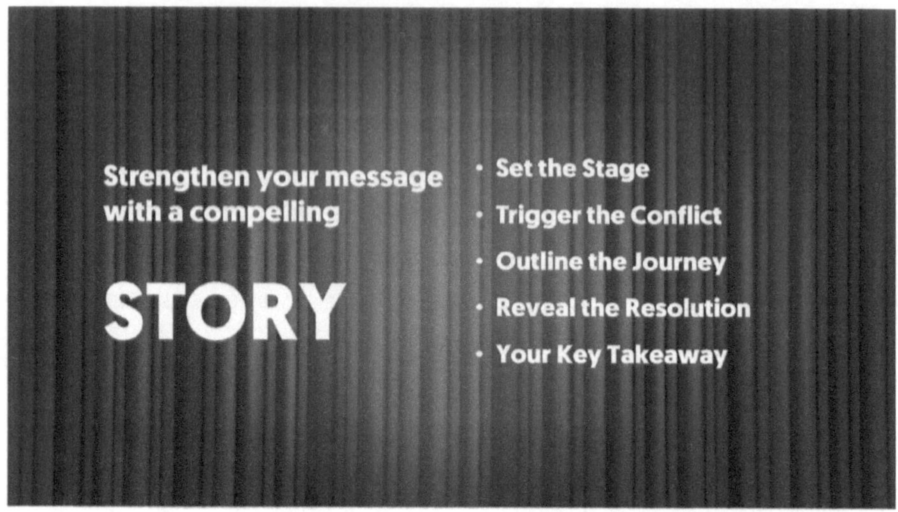

Rishi outlined the STORY framework, his tone encouraging.

"**Start with S—Set the Stage.** Establish the context and set the scene. This helps your audience understand the background and why the story matters."

"**Then, T – Trigger the Conflict**," Rishi continued. "Introduce the central conflict or challenge that needs to be addressed. This is what draws your audience in and makes them care about the outcome."

"**Next, O – Outline the Journey**," Rishi explained. "Take your audience through the steps taken to address the conflict. Show them the process, the struggles, and the progress made along the way."

Priya nodded, clearly engaged. "And then we reveal the resolution?"

"Exactly," Rishi said, smiling. "**R — Reveal the Resolution.** Conclude the story by revealing the outcome. Show how the conflict was resolved and what was achieved as a result."

"And finally, **Y — Your Key Takeaway**," Rishi added. "End with the key takeaway or moral of the story. This is what your audience should remember and apply moving forward."

Strengthen your message with a compelling STORY.

- Set the Stage
- Trigger the Conflict
- Outline the Journey
- Reveal the Resolution
- Your Key Takeaway

6.3.3 Expressing yourself CLEARly

Ram, his mind buzzing with new ideas, asked, "How do we make sure our writing is clear and to the point? We've struggled with being concise and keeping our messages focused."

Rishi nodded, understanding their concern. "That's where the next framework comes in. It's all about making your writing concise, logical, engaging, accurate, and responsive."

Rishi's tone became more instructional as he asked, "When you write, do you often find your message getting lost in long-winded explanations? Do you struggle to keep your arguments logical and easy to follow?"

Priya sighed, recognizing the truth in his words. "Yes, I sometimes get carried away with details and lose the main point."

"And that's a common challenge," Rishi said, his voice empathetic. "Let's talk about how to write a CLEAR copy."

Rishi began explaining the CLEAR framework in a measured tone: "Start by being Concise. Keep your messages clear and to the point. Don't overload your audience with unnecessary details."

"Then, make sure your arguments are Logical," Rishi continued. "Ensure that your points follow a logical flow, guiding your reader through your message in a way that makes sense."
Priya leaned in, eager to learn more. "What about keeping it engaging?"

"That's crucial," Rishi agreed. "Your content needs to be Engaging. Use compelling language, interesting examples, and a conversational tone to keep your reader's attention."

"And of course, it needs to be Accurate," Rishi added. "Provide accurate and well-researched information. Nothing undermines your credibility faster than factual errors."

"Finally, be Responsive," Rishi concluded. Tailor your message to your audience's needs and expectations. Make sure you're addressing their concerns and answering their questions."

To Sum-up:

- Concise: Keep your messages clear and to the point.
- Logical: Ensure your arguments follow a logical flow.
- Engaging: Make the content interesting and engaging.
- Accurate: Provide accurate and well-researched information.
- Responsive: Tailor your message to the needs and expectations of your audience.

6.3.4 Making your reports INSIGHTful

Feeling more confident, Priya asked, "How do we ensure that our reports and presentations are insightful, especially when dealing with data?"

Rishi's expression grew serious as he began to explain the INSIGHTful framework. "Being insightful is about more than just presenting data—it's about transforming that data into meaningful, actionable insights.

Many leaders struggle with this, particularly when data-driven decisions are overridden by gut feelings or the opinions of the highest-paid person in the room.

Rishi posed his next set of questions, his tone probing.

- "When you look at data, do you have a clear strategy for navigating it?
- Do you focus on the relevant datasets and filter out the noise?
- And once you have the data, do you know how to synthesize it into a coherent narrative that drives decision-making?"

Ram nodded, intrigued. "I've always thought that data speaks for itself, but I'm starting to see that it's how we interpret and present it that really matters."

"Exactly," Rishi said, leaning in. "Let's walk through the INSIGHTful framework."

Rishi began to outline the framework, his voice deliberate.

"Start by **Identifying Key Performance Indicators (KPIs)**. Define the key question or problem that needs to be addressed. Without a clear focus, it's easy to get lost in the data."

"Next, **Navigate the Data**," Rishi continued. "Dive into the data with a clear strategy, focusing on the relevant datasets and filtering out unnecessary information. This ensures that you're looking at the right information."

Priya leaned forward, clearly engaged. "And then we synthesize the information?"

"Exactly," Rishi replied. "**Synthesize Information** by combining data from different sources and perspectives to get a holistic view of the situation. This is where you start to see the bigger picture."

"Once you've synthesized the data," Rishi continued, "**Interpret the Findings**. Analyze the data to draw meaningful conclusions. Look for correlations, causations, and anomalies that can inform your decision-making."

"And then we generate insights, right?" Ram asked, his excitement growing.

"That's right," Rishi confirmed. "**Generate Insights** by transforming your findings into actionable insights that can guide strategic decisions. These insights should be clear, focused, and directly tied to the initial question."

"And don't forget to **Highlight the Implications**," Rishi added. "Understand the broader implications of your insights for the business or project. This is where you show why your insights matter."

"**Finally, Take Action**," Rishi concluded. "Develop a clear action plan based on the insights gathered. This is where you move from analysis to execution."

Rishi paused, letting the information settle before diving deeper. "

Understanding data is critical in today's business environment.

Data-driven leaders make decisions based on facts, not just intuition or the loudest voice in the room.

Unfortunately, in many organizations, the highest-paid person's opinion (HPPO) often overrides the team's insights, leading to decisions that are not grounded in reality."

Priya nodded, clearly understanding the importance of data-driven leadership. "So, it's about making sure the data drives the decision-making process, not just opinions."

"Exactly," Rishi agreed. "Data storytelling has become one of the most sought-after skills because it combines the analytical rigor of data with the emotional resonance of storytelling. When you can tell a compelling story with data, you're not just presenting numbers—you're influencing decisions and driving change."

As Rishi finished, Priya and Ram felt a renewed sense of purpose. They realized that by mastering the present, story, clear, and INSIGHTful frameworks, they could transform not only their written communication but also their ability to influence and lead.

To sum up

- Identify KPI
- Navigate the Data
- Synthesize Information
- Interpret the Findings.
- Generate Insights
- Highlight the Implications
- Take Action

6.4 The Art of verbal communication - Mastering communication layers, signals and collaboration

The late evening sun cast long shadows across the room as Priya and Ram sat across from Rishi, their minds still processing the wealth of knowledge they had absorbed.

But they knew one more crucial area they needed to master—oral communication.

They had experienced firsthand how easily misunderstandings could arise and were eager to learn how to communicate more effectively.

Priya broke the silence, her voice curious but determined. "Rishi, we've covered so much about organizing our work and improving our written communication, but what about our verbal communication?

We've had situations where even though we thought we were clear, things still got lost in translation."

Rishi, ever the seasoned guide, nodded thoughtfully. "Oral communication is an art in itself. It's not just about what you say, how you say it, and how you listen.

That's where several practical methods come in. These tools will help you navigate conversations more deeply, clearly, and effectively."

6.4.1. Mastering the communication LAYERS

Rishi leaned forward, his tone deliberate. "Let's start by analyzing the layers of a fruitful dialogue. This method is all about peeling back the layers of a conversation to get to the heart of the matter.

It's not just about hearing the words—it's about understanding their deeper meaning."

Rishi looked directly at Priya and Ram, his gaze intent.

- "When you're in a conversation, do you truly listen to what's being said, or do you find yourself jumping to conclusions?

- Are you able to pick up on the underlying emotions and messages, or do you sometimes miss the subtext?"

Ram nodded, acknowledging the challenge. "I've realized that I often focus on what's being said on the surface, but I miss the deeper meaning behind the words."

"And that's where the LAYERS framework comes in," Rishi said. "It helps you not just listen, but truly understand and engage with what's being communicated."

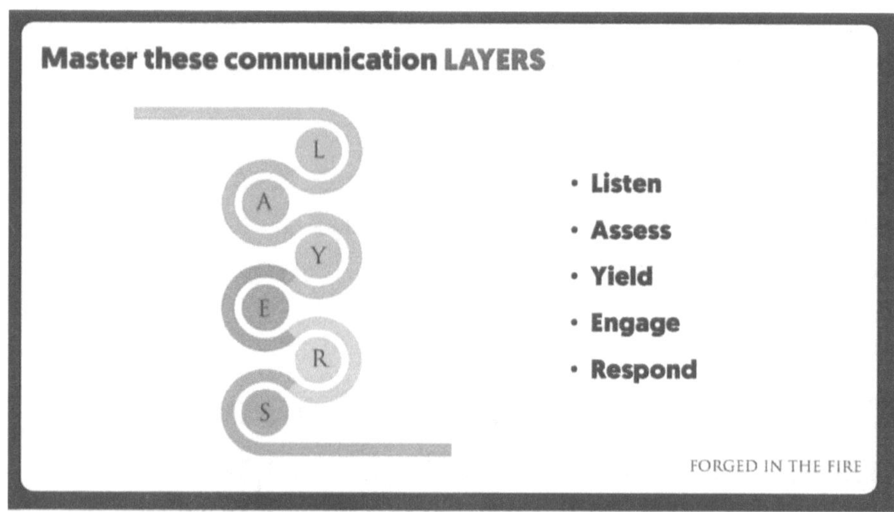

Rishi began to explain, his tone measured. "Start with **Listen.** Listen actively to what is being said without interrupting or planning your response while the other person is speaking."

"Next," he continued, "**Assess** the underlying messages and emotions. What is the other person trying to convey? What emotions are driving their words?"

Priya leaned in, her interest piqued. "So, it's not just about hearing the words, but about understanding the feelings behind them."

"Exactly," Rishi agreed. "Then you **Yield**. Give space for the other party to express fully without jumping in.

Sometimes, the most critical information comes after a pause, when the other person feels they have the room to continue."

"And then **Engage**," Rishi continued, "with the true meaning behind the words. Ask questions, clarify, and ensure you're on the same page. This deepens the conversation and shows that you're fully engaged."

"Finally," Rishi concluded, "**Respond** appropriately. Address both the surface and deeper layers of communication. Your response should reflect that you've understood the content and the emotion behind it."

- **Listen:** Listen actively to what is being said.
- **Assess:** Assess the underlying messages and emotions.
- **Yield:** Give space for the other party to express fully.
- **Engage:** Engage with the true meaning behind the words.
- **Respond:** Respond appropriately, addressing both the surface and deeper communication layers.

6.4.2 Sending the right SIGNALs

Feeling more confident, Priya asked, "What about nonverbal communication? How do we make sure we're sending the right signals?"

Rishi's expression grew thoughtful as he explained the SIGNALs framework: " Nonverbal communication is just as important as what you say.

It often speaks louder than words. The SIGNALs framework helps you improve your non-verbal communication, ensuring that your body language and gestures reinforce your verbal message."

Rishi leaned back in his chair, his tone thoughtful.

- "When you're in a conversation, are you aware of the non-verbal cues you're sending?
- Do you notice the body language of the person you're speaking with, and do you adjust your approach based on those signals?"

Ram nodded, intrigued. "I've always focused more on what's being said, but I'm realizing now that non-verbal communication plays a huge role in how the message is received."

6.4.2 Sending the right SIGNALs

"And you're right," Rishi agreed. "Let's break down the SIGNALs framework."

Rishi began to outline the framework, his voice steady. "Start with Show. Display confident body language—stand tall, make eye contact, and use open gestures. Your body language should project confidence and openness."

"Then," Rishi continued, "Interpret the non-verbal cues of others. Understand and read their body language—are they comfortable, engaged, or perhaps hesitant? This will guide how you proceed in the conversation."

Priya leaned forward, clearly engaged. "So it's about being aware of both our body language and that of the other person."

"Exactly," Rishi replied. "Next, Gesture purposefully. Use gestures to emphasize points, but ensure they're natural and not overdone. Your gestures should complement your words, not distract from them."

"And be sure to Neutralize negative signals," Rishi added. "Avoid closed body language like crossing your arms, which can come across as defensive or unapproachable. Instead, keep your posture open and inviting."

"Align your non-verbal signals with your verbal messages," Rishi continued. "Your body language should match what you're saying—if you're expressing confidence, your posture and gestures should reflect that."

"Finally," Rishi concluded, "Listen to your audience's nonverbal cues. Are they nodding, smiling, or leaning forward? These are signs that they're engaged. It might be time to adjust your approach if they're pulling back or seem disinterested."

To sum up...

- **Show**: Display confident body language.
- **Interpret**: Understand and read others' non-verbal cues.
- **Gesture**: Use gestures purposefully to emphasize points.
- **Neutralize**: Avoid negative non-verbal signals like closed posture.
- **Align**: Ensure your non-verbal signals align with your verbal messages.
- **Listen**: Be attentive to the non-verbal cues of your audience.

6.4.3 Fostering Collaboration

After a long day of exploring different frameworks, Priya and Ram felt excited and overwhelmed.

They sat with Rishi in his cottage's cozy, warmly lit living room, sipping on tea. The crackling sound of the fire in the background added a sense of calm to the intense learning session.

Priya leaned forward, resting her cup on the table. "Rishi, with everything we've learned so far, one thing still worries me—how do we pull the team together when we get back? We know the frameworks, but collaboration is always... tricky."

Ram nodded in agreement. "Yeah, getting everyone on the same page is hard, especially when everyone's so different."

Rishi smiled knowingly, setting his cup down. "That's a common challenge, but you're not alone. There's a framework designed specifically for that—one that ensures team collaboration is possible and productive. It's called COALESCE."

Priya tilted her head, intrigued. "COALESCE? What does it stand for?"

Rishi smiled and said, "It's an English word that roughly means 'coming together to form a group."

Rishi stood up, pacing slightly as he explained. "It's a framework that combines everything you need to collaborate effectively.

Each letter stands for a key element of successful teamwork." He paused, looking at them both to make sure they were following.

- **Connect:** Build rapport and trust among team members.
- **Organize:** Clearly define goals, roles, and responsibilities.
- **Align:** Ensure all team members are aligned with the common goals.
- **Leverage:** Utilize each team member's strengths.
- **Engage:** Keep team members motivated and actively involved.
- **Support:** Provide support when needed
- **Evaluate**: Assess the collaboration process and outcomes.
- **Co-create:** Encourage collective creativity and problem-solving.
- **Elevate:** Continuously improve the team's capabilities.

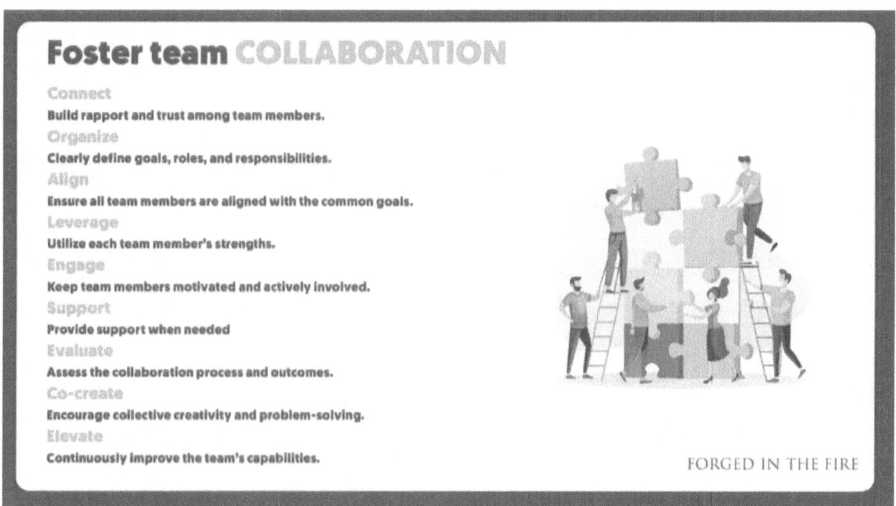

"First, you need to **Connect**. This means building trust and rapport with your team. You can't lead or collaborate with people without connection—without trust, the team will never fully open up."

Ram leaned back, thinking it through. "So, it's about understanding people beyond just their roles?"

"Exactly," Rishi nodded. "You need to know what motivates them and their strengths and weaknesses. That's the foundation."

Rishi continued, his voice calm but purposeful. "Next is **Organize**. Make sure goals, roles, and responsibilities are clearly defined.

People need to know their part in the bigger picture. Chaos happens when there's confusion about who's doing what."

Priya nodded. "That makes sense. I've seen projects derailed because no one knew their exact role."

"Precisely," Rishi agreed. "Then, we move to **Align**. Make sure everyone is working toward the same objective. Without alignment, even a well-organized team can fall apart if their individual goals don't match the team's overall mission."

Ram furrowed his brow, deep in thought. "So, that's like ensuring everyone's vision is synced with the company?"

"Yes," Rishi said, his eyes lighting up with approval. "Now, once you've aligned the team, you must **Leverage** their strengths. Not everyone is good at everything, so tap into what each team member excels at."

Priya grinned. "Like Ram's data analysis skills and my storytelling abilities?"

"Exactly!" Rishi laughed. "That's how you make the most of your team. But it's not enough to assign tasks and walk away.

You need to Engage them and keep them motivated and actively involved. Regular check-ins, feedback, and celebrations of small wins help maintain momentum."

Ram leaned forward, sipping his tea. "Right, because if people feel like they're just cogs in the machine, they disengage."

"Exactly," Rishi affirmed. "That's why you also need to support your team. Whether providing emotional support, additional resources, or simply being there to listen, your role as a leader is to ensure they don't feel lost or overwhelmed."

Priya raised her hand slightly, her curiosity piqued. "And what about after the project? What happens then?"

Rishi smiled, knowing this was the critical part. "You **Evaluate**. Take the time to assess what went well, what didn't, and where improvements can be made. This reflection helps the team learn and improve for future projects. No collaboration effort should go unexamined."

Priya and Ram exchanged glances, feeling more confident but still eager to understand the complete picture.

"So that's it?" Ram asked. "It ends with evaluation?"

"Not quite," Rishi said, pacing again. "The next step is to **Co-create**. This means encouraging the team to collaborate on solutions and ideas and fostering a culture of creativity.

The best teams don't just follow instructions—they innovate together."

"And the last part," Rishi continued, "is to **Elevate**. Always push for growth, both individually and as a team. Encourage personal development, new learning, and higher goals. Great teams are always striving to be better."

Ram and Priya both sat back, absorbing the information.

"So, COALESCE is really about ensuring that the team isn't just working together, but growing and innovating together," Priya said, a newfound determination in her voice.

Rishi smiled again, clearly proud of their understanding.

"Exactly. When you apply the COALESCE framework, you're not just managing a team—you're creating an environment where they can thrive."
Ram set his tea down, grinning. "Alright, I think we've got this. It's like putting all the pieces together in the right way."

Priya nodded, feeling the excitement build. "We're ready, Rishi."

Rishi looked at them both, his eyes twinkling with pride. "I know you are."

6.4.4 Having PEACEful conversations

Feeling more confident, Priya asked, "And what about handling situations when people are furious? We've had situations where emotions ran high, and things got heated. How do we communicate effectively in those moments?"

Rishi's expression grew firm as he began explaining the PEACE framework: "Conflict is inevitable, but how you handle it makes all the difference.

The PEACE framework is designed to help you excel in non-violent communication, ensuring that conflicts are resolved constructively."

Rishi's tone became more reflective as he asked,

- "When you're in a conflict, do you take a moment to calm down before responding, or do you react impulsively?

- Do you express your feelings clearly or hold back and let the tension build?"

Ram nodded, acknowledging the challenge. "I've realized that I often react too quickly, and it escalates the situation instead of resolving it."

"And that's where the PEACE framework comes in," Rishi said, his voice calm and steady. "Let's explore it together."

Rishi began to outline the **PEACE** framework, his voice soothing.

"Start with **Pause**. Take a moment to calm down before responding. This prevents knee-jerk reactions and gives you time to think."

"Then," Rishi continued, "**Express** your feelings clearly and without blame. It's important to communicate how you feel but do it in a way that doesn't attack the other person. Use 'I' statements instead of 'You' statements."

Priya leaned forward, clearly engaged. "And how do we consider the other person's perspective?"

"That's where **Ask** comes in," Rishi replied. "Ask for the other person's perspective. This shows you're willing to listen and understand their side of the story."

"And then **Collaborate**," Rishi continued. "Work together to find a mutually beneficial solution. This is about finding common ground and moving forward together."
"Finally," Rishi concluded, "**Empathize**. Show empathy and understanding throughout the conversation.

Recognize the other person's feelings and concerns are valid, even if you disagree. This helps to de-escalate tension and build a foundation for resolution."

As Rishi finished, Priya and Ram felt a newfound clarity and confidence.

They realized that mastering the SIGNALs, COALESCE, and PEACE frameworks could transform their verbal communication and their entire approach to leadership and collaboration.

Excel Non-Violent Communication with PEACE:

- **Pause**: Take a moment to calm down before responding.
- **Express**: Clearly express your feelings without blaming others.
- **Ask**: Ask for the other person's perspective.
- **Collaborate**: Work together to find a mutually beneficial solution.
- **Empathize**: Show empathy and understanding throughout the conversation.

6.5 Mastering Team Dynamics and Handling Special Situations

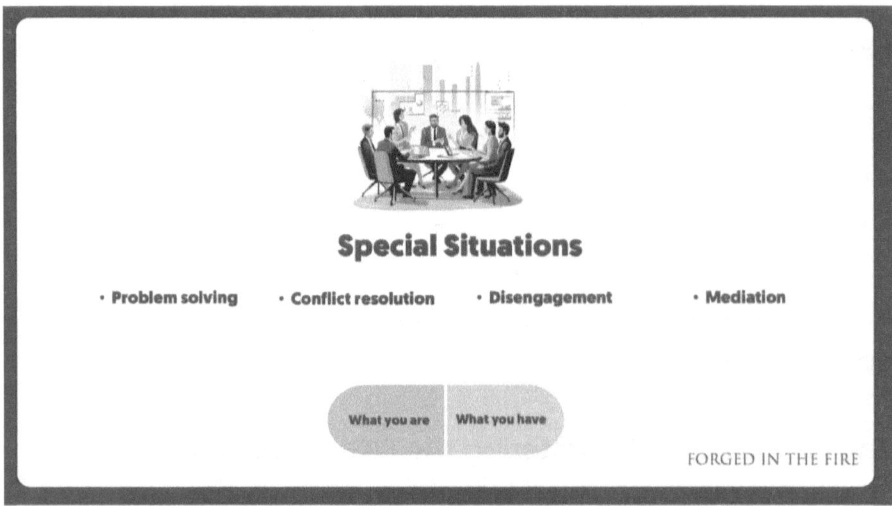

As the night deepened, Priya and Ram knew they were nearing the end of their intense learning session with Rishi.

The frameworks they had absorbed were already reshaping their approach to leadership and communication. But there was one final set of tools they needed to master—methods for managing teams, resolving conflicts, and navigating tough conversations.

Priya, ever the pragmatist, broke the silence. "Rishi, we've learned so much about communication and organization, but what about when things get really tough?

How do we handle conflict within the team, negotiate effectively, and ensure that we're all moving in the same direction?"

Rishi nodded, his expression serious. "Those are the situations that test your leadership the most. Whether you're resolving a conflict, guiding your team through a tough decision, or negotiating with stakeholders, you need a clear approach.

That's where these final frameworks come in. We will now cover various methods for mastering team dynamics and ensuring that you lead with both strength and empathy."

6.5.1 Getting everyone to CONCUR with you

Feeling more confident, Priya asked, "What about when we need to bring the team together, especially when there are differing opinions? How do we get everyone on the same page?"

Rishi nodded, recognizing the challenge. "That's where a simple method to have an accord with everyone comes in. It's about finding common ground, unifying views, and resolving conflicts effectively."

Rishi's tone became more reflective as he asked,

- "When there's a disagreement within your team, do you struggle to find a solution everyone can agree on?
- Do you feel like you sometimes force a compromise rather than find a proper consensus?"

Priya sighed, acknowledging the truth in his words. "It's hard to balance different perspectives, especially when emotions are involved."

"And that's where CONCUR can help," Rishi said, his voice reassuring. "Let's walk through it."

Rishi began to explain the CONCUR framework, his tone encouraging.

"Start with a firm **Commitment**. Ensure everyone is committed to finding a solution and moving forward together."

"Then," Rishi continued, "Appreciate the **Opposite** Perspective.

Take the time to understand where each person is coming from, even if you disagree. This builds empathy and respect."

Ram leaned in, eager to learn more. "And how do we find common ground?"

"That's where Identify **Needs** comes in," Rishi replied. "Identify the needs of both sides and look for areas of overlap. What do both parties want? What are their underlying concerns?"

"And then we try to unify views, right?" Priya asked, her interest growing.

"Exactly," Rishi agreed. "Find **Common** Ground and Try to **Unify Views**. Focus on the areas where you agree and build from there. This helps to create a sense of shared purpose."

"Finally," Rishi concluded, "**Reflect and Resolve**. Reflect on the process and make sure that everyone feels heard and valued. Then, work together to resolve the conflict and move forward as a unified team."

To sum up

- Start with a firm **COMMITMENT**
- Appreciate the **OPPOSITE** perspective

- Identify the **NEEDS** of both sides
- Find **COMMON** ground
- Try and **UNIFY** views
- Reflect and **RESOLVE**

6.5.2 Apply HEALER to your wounded team member

Feeling more confident, Ram asked, "How do we support our team members when they're struggling, especially emotionally?"

Rishi's expression grew serious as he began to explain the HEALER framework.

"Supporting your team through challenges requires empathy, understanding, and effective problem-solving.

The HEALER framework is designed to help you do just that."

Rishi's tone became more reflective as he asked,

- "When a team member is struggling, do you take the time to listen to their concerns?

- Do you offer practical and empathetic support, or do you sometimes feel like you're just going through the motions?"

Priya nodded, recognizing the challenge. "It's easy to get caught up in the tasks at hand and forget to connect with our team members personally."

"And that's where HEALER comes in," Rishi said, his voice calm and steady. "Let's explore it together."

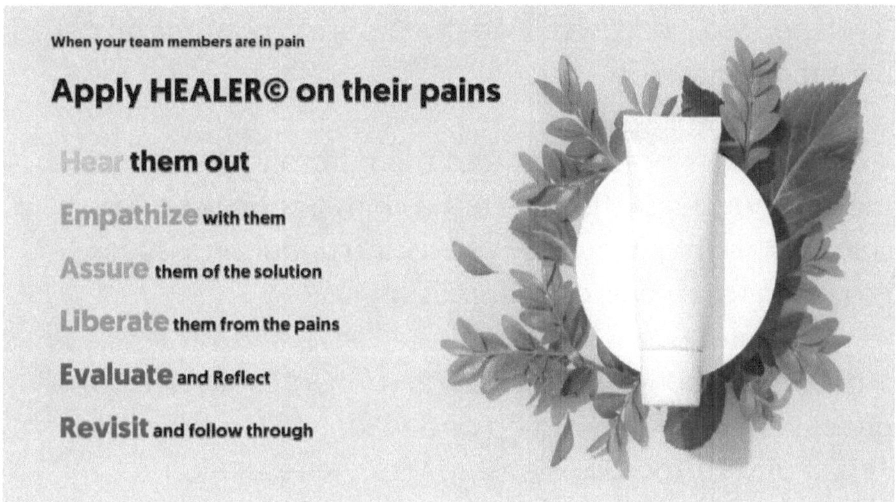

Rishi began to outline the HEALER framework, his voice soothing.

"Start by **Hearing** them out. Actively listen to ensure the team member feels understood. Sometimes, just being heard can make a world of difference."

"Then," Rishi continued, "**Empathize** with them. Show genuine empathy while maintaining emotional resilience.

It's essential to connect with their feelings without letting it overwhelm you."

Priya leaned forward, clearly engaged. "And how do we ensure we're helping them move forward?"

"That's where **Assure** them of the Solution comes in," Rishi replied. "Set realistic and achievable expectations for resolving the issue. Give them a sense of hope and direction."

"And then we work on solving the problem, right?" Ram asked, his interest growing.

"Exactly," Rishi agreed. "**Liberate** them from the Pains. Solve the root causes of the problem with thorough problem-solving. This might involve addressing underlying issues, providing resources, or offering support."

"Finally," Rishi concluded, "**Evaluate** and **Reflect**. Assess the effectiveness of the solution and reflect on the process. Revisit and Follow-Up to ensure that the resolution is sustained and that the team member feels supported."

To sum up…

- **Hear** them out
- **Empathize** with them
- **Assure** them of the solution
- **Liberate** them from the pains
- **Evaluate** and Reflect
- **Revisit** and follow through

6.5.3 NEGOTIATE better deals

Feeling more confident, Priya asked, "What about when we need to negotiate, whether it's with a client, a team member, or another stakeholder? How do we ensure a win-win outcome?"

Rishi nodded, recognizing the importance of negotiation. "That's where the NEGOTIATE framework comes in. It's about navigating needs, evaluating options, and reaching an agreement that benefits everyone involved."

Rishi's tone became more instructional as he asked,

- "When you enter a negotiation, do you clearly understand your needs and the needs of the other party?
- Do you approach the negotiation flexibly, or do you stick rigidly to your initial position?"

Ram sighed, acknowledging the truth in his words. "I've realized that I often go into negotiations focused on what I want rather than understanding what the other person needs."

"And that's where NEGOTIATE can help," Rishi said, his voice encouraging. "Let's break it down."

"Negotiation is a delicate balance," Rishi began, "but it's a skill that can make or break a deal. And to negotiate effectively, there are two key concepts you need to understand—BATNA and ZOPA."

Priya tilted her head slightly, her curiosity piqued. "I've heard those terms before, but I'm not sure I fully understand how to apply them."

Rishi smiled, always patient when explaining complex ideas. "Let's start with BATNA— **Best Alternative to a Negotiated Agreement.**

Consider it your fallback plan, the best option if the negotiation doesn't go your way."

Ram leaned forward, intrigued. "So, it's like knowing your backup strategy?"

"Exactly," Rishi nodded. "If the negotiation fails, what's your best alternative? For example, do you have other prospects lined up if you can't get the deal with this client? Knowing your BATNA gives you confidence because it tells you how much power you have in the negotiation.

The stronger your alternative, the more leverage you have."

Priya tapped her fingers on the table, processing the idea. "So if our fallback plan is weak, we'll feel more pressured to accept a bad deal?"

"Precisely," Rishi said. "That's why developing a solid BATNA is critical before any negotiation.

If you know you have a solid alternative, you're less likely to make compromises that don't align with your goals."

Ram nodded, already thinking ahead. "Okay, got it. And what about ZOPA?"

"Ah, ZOPA—the Zone of Possible Agreement," Rishi continued.

"This is the range where both parties can find common ground. It's the overlap between what you're willing to accept and what the other party is willing to offer. If there's no overlap, there's no deal."

Priya leaned forward, frowning slightly. "How do you figure out what their range is?"

Rishi smiled, knowing this was a critical question. "That's where research and understanding your counterpart comes in.

You need to anticipate their BATNA as well. What are their limits? What's the minimum they'd accept? Once you understand their position, you can work to find the ZOPA— that space where both sides can agree."

Ram, ever the strategist, furrowed his brow. "So, if our acceptable range and their acceptable range don't overlap, we walk away?"

"Exactly," Rishi confirmed. "If there's no ZOPA, it's better to walk away and rely on your BATNA. But the negotiation is successful if you can find that sweet spot where both sides' interests meet."

Priya's eyes lit up as the concept clicked. "So, we're not just negotiating blindly. We're looking for that range—finding where our interests align with theirs."

"Exactly," Rishi said, his tone encouraging. "Negotiation is about understanding both your limits and the other party's. Once you know your BATNA and have identified the ZOPA, you can approach the negotiation clearly and confidently."

Ram leaned back, a smile crossing his face. "That makes a lot of sense. If we know where the common ground is, we'll be in control."

"Exactly," Rishi replied, pleased with their understanding.

"Negotiation isn't about forcing your will on someone. It's about finding a solution that benefits both parties—within the boundaries of your BATNA and ZOPA."

Priya smiled, the anxiety from earlier melting away. "Thanks, Rishi. I think we've got this."

Rishi began to explain the NEGOTIATE framework, his tone steady. "Start with **Navigate** the Needs. Understand your needs and the other party's to focus on value creation. This is about finding a solution that benefits both sides."

"Then," Rishi continued, "**Evaluate** your BATNA. Assess your best alternative to a negotiated agreement before entering negotiations. This ensures that you negotiate from a position of strength."

Priya leaned in, eager to learn more. "And how do we find common ground?"

"That's where **Gauge** the ZOPA comes in," Rishi replied

"And then we work towards a win-win outcome, right?" Ram asked, his interest growing.

"Exactly," Rishi agreed. "**Open** with Win-Win in Mind. Start with a collaborative mindset to create mutually beneficial outcomes. This sets the tone for a positive negotiation."

"Next," Rishi continued, "**Test Assumptions** and Proposals. Clarify assumptions and explore proposals to uncover hidden interests and opportunities. This ensures that both sides understand each other's positions."

"Then," Rishi said, "**Identify** Common Ground. Find areas of agreement early to build momentum in the negotiation. This helps to create a sense of progress and cooperation."

"Finally," Rishi concluded, "**Adjust** and Adapt. Be flexible and adapt your approach as the negotiation progresses.

Then, **Tie Up** the Agreement by clearly outlining and confirming the terms to ensure alignment. Evaluate the Outcome to reflect on the negotiation process and learn from it."

To sum up..

- **Navigate** the Needs
- **Evaluate** Your BATNA
- **Gauge** the ZOPA
- **Open** with Win-Win in Mind
- **Test** Assumptions and Proposals
- **Identify** Common Ground
- **Adjust** and Adapt
- **Tie** Up the Agreement
- **Evaluate** the Outcome

6.5.4 Having CRUCIAL conversations

Feeling more confident, Ram asked, "What about handling tough conversations? How do we ensure that we approach them with care and effectiveness?"

Rishi nodded, recognizing the importance of this skill. "That's where the CRUCIAL framework comes in. It's designed to help you navigate difficult conversations with clarity, respect, and effectiveness."

Rishi's tone became more instructional as he asked,

- "When you need to have a difficult conversation, do you take the time to clarify your purpose before diving in?
- Do you respect the emotions involved and ensure that the other person's perspective is understood?"

Priya sighed, acknowledging the truth in his words. "It's hard to stay calm and focused during tough conversations, especially when emotions run high."

"And that's where CRUCIAL can help," Rishi said, his voice encouraging. "Let's break it down."

Rishi began to explain the CRUCIAL framework, his tone steady.

"Start with **Clarify** the Purpose. Understand what you want to achieve from the conversation and stay focused on that goal."

"Then," Rishi continued, "**Respect** Emotions. Recognize that emotions are an integral part of tough conversations and approach them with sensitivity."

Ram leaned in, eager to learn more. "And how do we make sure we're considering the other person's perspective?"

"That's where **Understand** Their Perspective comes in," Rishi replied. "Listen actively and ensure you fully understand their point of view before responding."

"And then we communicate our perspective, right?" Priya asked, her interest growing.

"Exactly," Rishi agreed. "**Communicate** Your Perspective clearly and respectfully. Ensure you express your thoughts and feelings without blaming or attacking."

"Next," Rishi said, "**Identify** Common Ground. Look for areas where you agree and build on those to create a shared purpose."

"Finally," Rishi concluded, "**Agree** on Actions. Decide on the next steps together and ensure that both parties are committed to following through.

Look Back and Reflect on the conversation to learn from it and improve future interactions."

To sum up

- **Clarify** the Purpose.
- **Recognize** and Respect Emotions.
- **Understand** Perspectives
- **Communicate** Your needs
- **Identify** Common Ground.
- **Agree** on Actions.
- **Look** Back and Reflect

6.5.5 Dealing with DELICATE issues

Feeling more confident, Priya asked, "And what about when we're dealing with really sensitive issues? How do we approach those conversations delicately?"

Rishi's expression grew serious as he began to explain the DELICATE framework. "Sensitive conversations require an extra level of care and consideration.

The DELICATE framework is designed to help you navigate these discussions with empathy and respect."

Rishi's tone became more reflective as he asked,

- "When you're dealing with a sensitive issue, do you take the time to define the problem clearly and empathize with the emotions involved?

- Do you ensure you're listening actively and informing the other person?"

Ram nodded, recognizing the challenge. "It's easy to get caught up in the moment's emotions and lose sight of the need for clarity and empathy."

"And that's where DELICATE comes in," Rishi said, his voice calm and steady. "Let's explore it together."

Rishi began to outline the DELICATE framework, his voice thoughtful. "Start with **Define** the Issue. Make sure that you're clear on what the issue is and why it's important."

"Then," Rishi continued, "**Empathize** with Emotions. Show genuine empathy for the feelings involved and ensure the other person knows you understand their perspective."

Priya leaned forward, clearly engaged. "And how do we make sure we're listening and communicating effectively?"

"That's where **Listen** Actively comes in," Rishi replied. "Ensure that you're fully present and engaged in the conversation, without interrupting or judging."

"And then we inform the other person, right?" Ram asked, his interest growing.

"Exactly," Rishi agreed. "**Inform** with Clarity. Make sure that your message is clear, concise, and respectful."

"Next," Rishi said, "**Collaborate** on Solutions. Work together to find a resolution that addresses the issue while respecting the emotions involved."

"And finally," Rishi concluded, "**Agree** on Next Steps and Take Time to Reflect. Ensure that both parties are committed to the agreed-upon actions and take time to reflect on the conversation to learn and grow from it.

Evaluate the Outcome to ensure that the resolution is effective and sustainable."

To sum up

- **Define** the Issue.
- **Empathize** with emotions.
- **Listen** actively
- **Inform** with clarity
- **Collaborate** on solutions
- **Agree** on next steps
- **Take** time to reflect

As Rishi finished, Priya and Ram felt a newfound sense of confidence and clarity.

They realized that mastering communication to handle special situations is super helpful.

With the newly acquired skillsets. they could lead their team through even the most challenging situations with strength, empathy, and effectiveness.

6.6 Critical enablers of communication

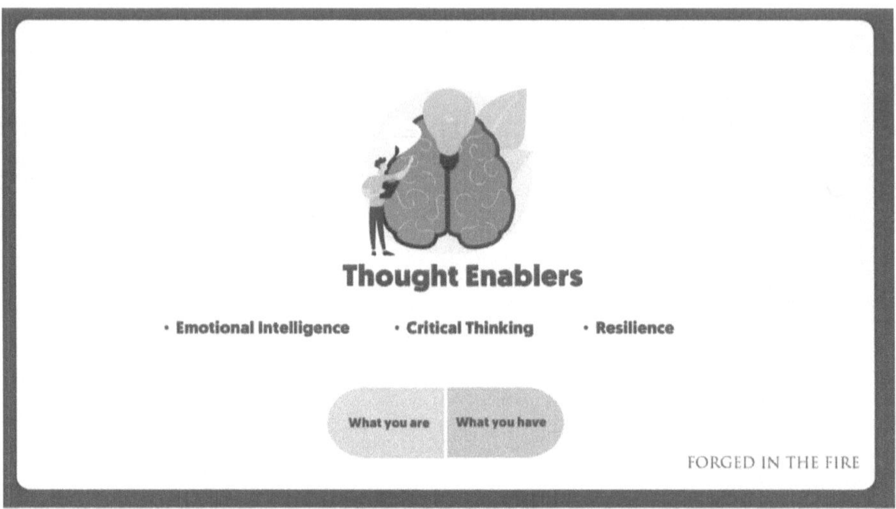

The morning session had been intense but illuminating. Priya and Ram had spent hours delving into Rishi's meticulously laid out communication frameworks.

The frameworks felt powerful in their hands, like new tools that could reshape their approach to leadership and problem-solving. Yet, Rishi knew they needed something more to wield these tools effectively.

As the discussion on the last framework wrapped up, Rishi leaned back in his chair, his gaze steady on Priya and Ram.

He could see the wheels turning in their minds, the quiet determination beginning to settle in. But he also knew they weren't quite there yet.

"Now that you've got a solid grasp of the communication frameworks," Rishi began, his tone serious but encouraging, "it's time to introduce you to **three critical enablers**—skills that will help you apply these frameworks more effectively and navigate any special or adverse situations you might encounter."

Priya tilted her head slightly, curiosity sparking in her eyes. "Critical enablers?"

"Exactly," Rishi confirmed. "These enablers are like the foundation beneath a house.

They're not always visible, but they're essential for everything else to stand strong. The three we're going to focus on are Emotional Intelligence, Critical Thinking, and Resilience.

Mastering these will elevate your ability to use the frameworks and help you stay grounded, no matter what challenges come your way."

Ram leaned forward, eager to learn more. "So, these enablers will help us not just understand the frameworks but also apply them better, especially in tough situations?"

"Precisely," Rishi said with a nod. "Let's start with the first enabler—Emotional Intelligence."

Emotional Intelligence – The Foundation of Effective Leadership

Rishi's voice took on a deliberate, measured tone as he continued. "Emotional Intelligence is about understanding and managing your own emotions while also being attuned to the feelings of others.

It allows you to navigate complex interpersonal dynamics, remain calm under pressure, and connect with people on a deeper level."

Priya's brow furrowed slightly as she considered the concept.

"But how does this tie into the frameworks we've just learned?"

Rishi smiled slightly. "Think of Emotional Intelligence as the glue that holds everything together.

When you practice frameworks like PEACE or COALESCE, your ability to understand and manage emotions—both yours and others'—i what makes those frameworks truly effective.

It's the difference between simply applying a technique and genuinely connecting with people, which leads to lasting solutions."

He continued, laying out the critical components of Emotional Intelligence: "Self-Awareness, Self-Management, Social Awareness, and Relationship Management.

Each of these components supports the frameworks you've learned by ensuring you're not just reacting to situations but responding thoughtfully and with empathy."

Next, **Critical Thinking** – The Key to Sharp Decision-Making Rishi paused, letting the importance of Emotional Intelligence settle before moving on.

"The second enabler is Critical Thinking. This is your ability to analyze situations objectively, evaluate information critically, and make decisions based on logic rather than impulse."

Ram nodded, understanding the connection. "So, it's about applying the frameworks not just by rote but by really thinking through each step, right?"

"Exactly," Rishi affirmed. "Critical Thinking ensures that when you're using frameworks like SSOLVER or INSIGHTful, you're not just going through the motions.

You're actively questioning, analyzing, and making informed decisions. This helps you see beyond the obvious, anticipate challenges, and develop robust and well-thought-out strategies."

Priya leaned in, her interest piqued. "And this ties into our ability to handle complex or unexpected situations, doesn't it?"

"It does," Rishi agreed. "Critical Thinking allows you to adapt and pivot when things are unplanned. It's the skill that helps you cut through the noise and focus on what matters."

Resilience – The Strength to Keep Going

Rishi's expression softened slightly as he introduced the final enabler. "The third enabler is Resilience. This is your ability to bounce back from setbacks, to keep pushing forward even when the odds are against you."

Priya and Ram both nodded, the significance of this enabler not lost on them. They had already faced setbacks and knew there would be more ahead.

"Resilience," Rishi continued, " keeps you going when things get tough.

When using frameworks like CHANGE or HEALER, resilience allows you to maintain your focus and determination even when faced with adversity.

It's about not giving up, about finding the strength within yourself to push through challenges and come out stronger on the other side."

Ram's voice was quiet but filled with resolve. "So, these enablers will help us not just survive but thrive, no matter what comes our way."

Rishi nodded, a small smile playing on his lips. "Exactly. Emotional Intelligence will help you connect and communicate effectively.

Critical Thinking will sharpen your decision-making and problem-solving abilities.

And Resilience will give you the strength to persevere, no matter how difficult the journey."

He leaned forward, his voice filled with quiet conviction. "These enablers will turn the frameworks you've learned from tools into powerful assets. Master them, and you won't just be prepared for the challenges of this project—you'll be ready for whatever life throws your way."

Priya and Ram exchanged a look, the weight of Rishi's words sinking in.

They knew mastering these enablers would require dedication and practice, but they were ready.

With a renewed sense of purpose, they realized that they were learning to succeed in life, not just in a project.

6.6.1 Building Emotional Intelligence

The cottage was filled with a gentle hum of nature, the rustling leaves outside, and the occasional call of birds, creating a peaceful backdrop to the intense conversation inside.

Priya and Ram sat across from Rishi, their notebooks open, ready to absorb every bit of wisdom he was about to share.

Rishi leaned forward, his expression thoughtful yet determined. "We've talked about Emotional Intelligence as one of the critical enablers, but now it's time to dive deeper.

This is not just a concept—it's a skill you must practice and master. It will allow you to connect deeply with others, manage your emotions, and lead effectively under any circumstances."

Priya nodded; her pen poised to take notes. "I'm ready, Rishi. How do we start?"

Rishi smiled slightly, appreciating her eagerness. "Let's break it down into four key components.

Mastering these will not only make you better leaders but will also improve every interaction you have, whether in the workplace or in your personal lives."

1. Self-Awareness – The First Step to Mastery

Rishi began with a calm yet firm tone. "The foundation of Emotional Intelligence is Self-Awareness.

This is your ability to recognize your emotions, understand their triggers, and see how they influence your thoughts and behavior. Without self-awareness, you can't hope to manage your emotions effectively."

Ram leaned in, curious. "How do we develop self-awareness?"

Rishi's gaze was steady. "It starts with reflection. Throughout your day, take moments to check in with yourself. Ask, 'What am I feeling right now, and why?' Don't just brush off emotions—examine them.

Are you feeling stressed, angry, or excited? Identify what triggered those emotions. Was it a comment from a colleague, a looming deadline, or something personal?"

Priya nodded, already seeing how this could be useful. "So, it's about being in tune with our emotions instead of just letting them pass by unnoticed."

"Exactly," Rishi agreed. "The more you practice this, the better you'll catch your emotions in the moment. This awareness is the first step in gaining control over how you react."

1.   Self-Management – The Power to Choose Your Response

Rishi continued; his tone more deliberate. "Once you're aware of your emotions, Self-Management is next. This is your ability to control and manage your emotions, especially in stressful situations."

Ram looked thoughtful. "It sounds challenging, especially in the heat of the moment."

"It can be," Rishi acknowledged. "But it's also where you find your true strength. Self-management is about not letting your emotions dictate your actions.

It's about choosing how you respond. When you feel anger rising, you pause instead of snapping at someone. Take a deep breath. Count to ten if you need to. Give yourself a moment to think before you react."

Priya smiled, the practicality of it resonating with her. "**So it's not about suppressing emotions but constructively managing them**."

"Exactly," Rishi confirmed. "Techniques like deep breathing, taking a short walk to clear your head, or even mentally stepping back to reframe the situation can help. It's about staying composed, especially when the pressure is on."

2. Social Awareness – Understanding Others

Rishi's voice softened as he moved on to the next component. "Next is Social Awareness. This is your ability to understand the emotions of others.

It's about being attuned to the emotional currents around you—whether in a team meeting, a one-on-one conversation, or even in a casual setting."

Priya's brow furrowed slightly. "How do we get better at that?"

"Start by paying attention," Rishi advised. "Observe people's body language, tone of voice, and facial expressions.

What are they really feeling? Sometimes, what someone says isn't the whole story. They might say they're fine, but their body language might tell you they're stressed or upset.

The more you practice tuning into these signals, the better you'll become at understanding others' emotions."

Ram nodded slowly, seeing the connection. "And this helps us respond more appropriately, right? If we understand what someone is really feeling, we can address their concerns more effectively."

"Exactly," Rishi said. "Social Awareness helps you navigate complex interpersonal situations with empathy and insight. It's the key to building trust and rapport with others."

4. Relationship Management – Building Strong, Positive Connections

Rishi leaned back slightly, letting the significance of the final component settle in. "The last component is Relationship Management.

This is where all the other components come together. **It's about using self-awareness, self-management, and social awareness to build strong, positive relationships with others."**

Priya's eyes brightened with understanding. "So, it's about applying everything we've learned to interact more effectively with others?"

"Exactly," Rishi affirmed. "Relationship Management involves clear communication, active listening, and influencing and inspiring others. **It's about resolving conflicts constructively, leading with empathy, and ensuring that your interactions leave a positive impact."**

Ram leaned forward, his voice filled with determination. "And this makes a leader effective—not just getting results, but building strong, trusting relationships along the way."

"Yes," Rishi said with a nod. "A leader who masters Emotional Intelligence is not just a manager of tasks, but a builder of people. By practicing these four components, you'll find that your ability to connect with and lead others will transform."

Putting Emotional Intelligence into Practice

Rishi paused, letting the weight of his words sink in. "Now that you understand the components, it's time to put them into practice.

Start small—maybe by reflecting on your emotions at the end of each day or by paying closer attention to the feelings of those around you. The more you practice, the more natural it will become."

Priya and Ram exchanged glances, both feeling the importance of what they had just learned.

"Remember," Rishi concluded, "Emotional Intelligence isn't a destination—it's a journey. The more you work on it, the better you'll be at navigating the complexities of leadership, communication, and life. It's a skill that will serve you in every aspect of your life, helping you succeed and thrive."

With that, Rishi leaned back, signaling the end of the session.

Priya and Ram felt a sense of clarity and purpose. They knew that mastering Emotional Intelligence would be key to their growth, and they were ready to start practicing, one step at a time.

The room was filled with a sense of quiet determination as Priya and Ram absorbed Rishi's outlined key components of Emotional Intelligence. They understood its importance, but they were also eager to know how to apply these concepts to their daily lives.

Rishi could sense their readiness to take the next step.

He leaned forward slightly, his tone becoming more instructive. "Understanding Emotional Intelligence is the first step, but like any skill, it needs to be practiced consistently to become a natural part of who you are. Let's talk about how you can start practicing EI in your daily life."

1. Practicing Self-Awareness

Rishi began with a calm, guiding tone. "The first component, Self-Awareness, is something you can start practicing immediately. It's about becoming more in tune with your emotions and how they influence your thoughts and actions."

Ram nodded, eager to learn. "What's the best way to start?"

Rishi smiled slightly, appreciating his enthusiasm. "Start by setting aside a few minutes at different points during the day to check in with yourself.

This could be when you wake up, before a meeting, or at the end of the day.

Ask yourself, 'What am I feeling right now? Why am I feeling this way?' Don't judge the emotions—observe them."

Priya took notes, and her mind was already planning how to incorporate this into her routine. "So, it's about pausing and reflecting on our emotional state, even amid a busy day."

"Exactly," Rishi confirmed. "Another powerful tool is journaling. Please spend a few minutes at the end of each day writing about your emotions, what triggered them, and how you responded.

This helps you process your feelings and reveals patterns over time. You'll start to see what consistently triggers certain emotions and how you typically respond."

2. Practicing Self-Management

Rishi moved on to the next component, his voice steady. "Self-management is about taking control of your emotions, especially in stressful situations. Here's how you can practice it."

Ram listened intently. "What should we focus on?"

Rishi continued, "The next time you feel a strong emotion—anger, frustration, or anxiety—take a moment to pause.

Instead of reacting immediately, practice a technique like deep breathing. Inhale slowly for a count of four, hold for four, and then exhale for four.

This simple act can help calm your nervous system and allow you to choose a more measured response."

Priya looked intrigued. "So, it's about creating a gap between feeling and reacting."

"Exactly," Rishi agreed. "You can also try reframing negative thoughts. If you think, 'I can't handle this,' consciously replace it with, 'This is challenging, but I can figure it out.' Over time, this practice will help you build emotional resilience and respond to situations more calmly and clearly."

3. Practicing Social Awareness

Rishi's tone softened as he addressed the next area. "Social Awareness is about tuning into the emotions of those around you. Here's how you can start practicing it."

Priya leaned in, curious. "How do we become more socially aware?"

"Start by paying attention," Rishi said. "In your next meeting or conversation, focus on the spoken words and non-verbal cues.

What's the tone of voice? What's the body language saying? Are they avoiding eye contact, or are they fidgeting? These small details can give you insight into the other person's feelings."

Ram nodded, seeing the value. "It's about reading between the lines."

"Exactly," Rishi confirmed. "You can also practice empathy by putting yourself in another person's shoes.

Ask yourself, 'How would I feel if I were in their situation?' This helps you connect with others on a deeper level and respond in more understanding and supportive ways."

4. Practicing Relationship Management

Rishi leaned back slightly, letting the significance of the final component settle in. "Finally, Relationship Management is about using your emotional intelligence to build and maintain strong, positive relationships."

Priya's eyes brightened with understanding. "How do we practice this in our daily interactions?"

"One way," Rishi began, "is by practicing active listening. When you're in a conversation, focus entirely on the speaker.

Don't just wait for your turn to speak—listen. Acknowledge their points, ask clarifying questions, and show that you value their perspective."

Ram looked thoughtful. "So, it's about making others feel heard and understood."

"Yes," Rishi agreed. "Another critical practice is giving constructive feedback. When you need to address an issue with someone, do it in a clear and supportive way.

Use 'I' statements instead of 'You' statements to avoid sounding accusatory. For example, say, 'I noticed that the project was delayed, and I'm concerned about how we can improve our process,' instead of, 'You didn't finish on time.' This keeps the conversation focused on solutions rather than blame."

Priya took a deep breath, feeling both the weight and the value of what Rishi was saying. "These practices seem simple, but I can see how they would make a big difference." "They do," Rishi confirmed. "The key is consistency. Emotional Intelligence isn't something you develop overnight.

It's a skill that requires ongoing practice. But the more you work on it, the more naturally it will come to you, and the more effective you'll become as a leader and as a person."

Putting It All Together

Rishi's voice took on a final note of encouragement.

"Start small. Pick one practice to focus on each week—maybe it's checking in with your emotions at the end of each day or actively listening during meetings.
Over time, you can build on these practices until they become second nature."

He leaned forward, his gaze steady on both Priya and Ram.

"Remember, emotional intelligence is the foundation that supports everything else you do.

It will enhance your ability to apply the frameworks we've discussed, navigate complex situations, and build meaningful relationships. It's a lifelong journey that will pay off in every area of your life."

Priya and Ram exchanged determined glances, their minds already set on incorporating these practices into their daily routines. They knew mastering Emotional Intelligence would be a game-changer—not just for the project at hand but for their future success as leaders.

6.6.2 Unveiling the Enablers - CRITICal Thinking

The sun had climbed higher in the sky, casting warm light through the windows of Rishi's cottage.

Priya and Ram were deep in thought, their minds still processing the insights they had gained on Emotional Intelligence. But Rishi knew there was another key enabler they needed to master: **Critical Thinking**.

Rishi stood up, pacing slightly as he prepared to introduce this next vital skill. "Now that we've covered Emotional Intelligence, it's time to move on to something equally important but often misunderstood—Critical Thinking."

Ram looked up; curiosity evident in his eyes. "I've always heard about the importance of Critical Thinking, but honestly, it sounds a bit dry. How do we make it practical and useful?"

Rishi chuckled, understanding the sentiment. "You're right, Ram. Critical Thinking can seem abstract, but let me tell you, it's anything but dry when you're using it in real life.

Think of it as the ability to navigate through the fog of uncertainty, to see clearly when assumptions or biases might blind others. It's what separates a good decision from a great one."

The Chess Master's Mind

Rishi stopped pacing and turned to face them, his expression severe but engaging. "Let me start with an analogy. Imagine a chess master playing a game. To the untrained eye, it looks like they're simply moving pieces around a board. But in reality, the chess master is thinking several moves ahead, considering all possible outcomes before deciding. They're analyzing the entire board, not just the immediate situation in front of them."

Priya's eyes lit up with understanding. "So, Critical Thinking is about seeing the bigger picture and not just reacting to what's right in front of you."

"Exactly," Rishi confirmed. "It's about gathering all the relevant information, questioning assumptions, evaluating options, and then making a decision that's not just based on what's happening now, but on what could happen next.

It's a skill that allows you to anticipate consequences and adapt your strategy accordingly."

The Pilot's Dilemma

Rishi continued, leaning forward slightly to draw them in. "Let me share a story to illustrate this.

There's an old tale about a commercial pilot flying through a storm. The weather was rough, and visibility was low.

The panel instruments gave conflicting readings, and the co-pilot panicked, unsure of what to trust. But the experienced and calm pilot didn't just react to the situation. Instead, he paused, assessed the information critically, and decided based on what he knew was most reliable. That decision saved the flight.

Ram leaned in, clearly engaged. "So, the pilot didn't just go with the first thing that came to mind. He evaluated the situation carefully."

"Exactly," Rishi said. "Critical Thinking is like that pilot's skill. It's about not letting pressure or confusion cloud your judgment.

Instead, you step back, gather all the relevant data, question what seems off, and then make a well-reasoned decision. It's the difference between reacting impulsively and responding thoughtfully."

Rishi's tone became more instructive as he transitioned to practical applications. "So, how do you develop this skill? Let me break it down into practical steps you can use immediately."

Rishi leaned forward with a slight smile as he prepared to share his idea. "Now that we've covered the key steps of Critical Thinking, I want to introduce a simple tool to help you remember and apply these steps whenever necessary.

The term I've chosen is one you're already familiar with— CRITIC."

Priya's interest was piqued. "CRITIC? That's clever. How does it work?"

"Exactly," Rishi said with a nod. "CRITIC is an acronym that captures the essence of Critical Thinking. Each letter stands for a step in the process."

Ram leaned in, eager to hear more. "This sounds like something we can use right away."

Rishi began to explain the breakdown of CRITIC:

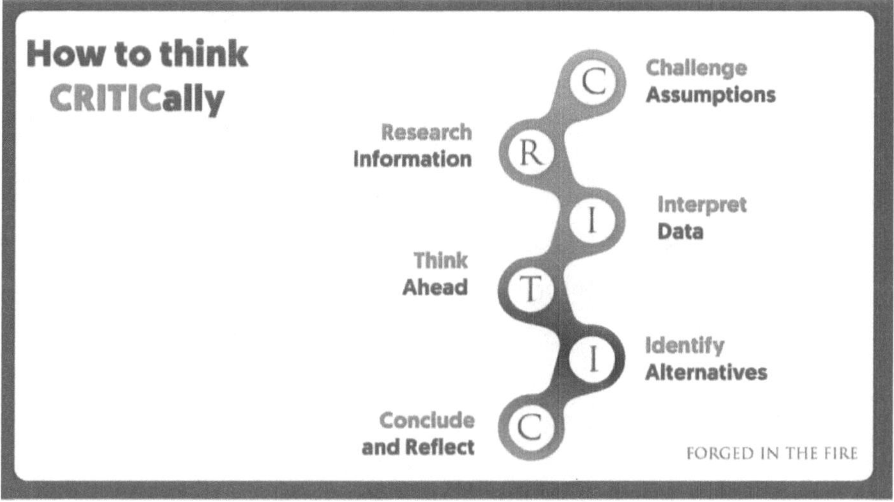

- **Challenge Assumptions:** "Start by challenging your assumptions. Don't take things at face value. Ask yourself, 'What am I assuming here, and is it valid?' This helps you avoid biases and think more objectively."

- **Research Information:** "Next, research thoroughly. Gather relevant data from multiple sources and perspectives. Don't rely on just one point of view—dig deeper to get a comprehensive understanding."

- **Interpret Data:** "Once you've gathered the information, interpret it critically. Analyze the data, cross-check your sources, and determine what's reliable. Look for patterns, inconsistencies, and insights."

- **Think Ahead:** "Always think ahead to the consequences of your decisions. Consider the short-term and long-term impacts. What might happen as a result of this choice? How will it affect others?"

- **Identify Alternatives:** "Before settling on a decision, identify and consider alternatives. What other options are available? How do they compare to your current choice? This step helps you avoid tunnel vision."

- **Conclude and Reflect:** "Finally, conclude by making a decision and then reflect on the process. After you've seen the outcome, take the time to review what worked well and what could be improved. This reflection helps you refine your Critical Thinking skills for the future."

Priya smiled, already seeing how useful this would be. "CRITIC—it's perfect. It's easy to remember and ties directly to the idea of Critical Thinking."

Ram nodded in agreement. "And it covers all the steps we need to make better decisions. This is something we can use every day."

"Exactly," Rishi said, pleased with their response. "Whenever you're faced with a decision or problem, think CRITIC and be your critic.

It will guide you through the process, ensuring your approach is thorough, thoughtful, and strategic."

Priya and Ram exchanged glances, their minds thinking about how to apply these principles in their work and personal lives.

Rishi gave them a reassuring smile. "Remember, Critical Thinking is your tool for cutting through the noise and making decisions that are not just reactive but proactive. It's the skill that will help you navigate complexity, solve problems creatively, and lead with clarity."

As they left the session, Priya and Ram felt a new sense of purpose. They knew mastering Critical Thinking would be crucial to their success—not just in their current project but in all the challenges ahead.

The discussion on Critical Thinking had been enlightening, but Rishi knew that remembering each step might still be challenging for Priya and Ram in the heat of the moment.

He had an idea that would help make these steps memorable and inherently related to Critical Thinking.

As the session concluded, Priya and Ram felt renewed confidence. With CRITIC as their guide, they knew they had a reliable tool to help them navigate the complexities of decision-making in their careers and personal lives.

6.6.3 Unveiling the Enablers - Resilience

The sun was now at its peak, casting a bright light through the windows of Rishi's cottage. Priya and Ram, feeling invigorated by their new understanding of Emotional Intelligence and Critical Thinking, were ready to tackle the final enabler Rishi had promised to teach them—Resilience.

Rishi could see the determination in their eyes, but he knew their journey would not always be smooth. Challenges and setbacks were inevitable, and how they responded to those would determine their authentic success. He leaned forward, his tone severe but warm.

"We've covered a lot today," Rishi began, "but there's one more critical enabler you need to master—Resilience. This is your ability to bounce back from setbacks, to keep pushing forward even when the odds are against you."

Priya nodded thoughtfully. "I've always admired resilient people, but I've never really understood how to cultivate it myself."

"Resilience," Rishi explained, "is not something you're born with or without. It's a skill, just like the others we've discussed. And it's essential—not just for your career but your entire life. Let me start with an analogy."

Rishi picked up a rubber band from his desk and held it out for them to see. "Think of resilience like a rubber band.

When you stretch it, it bends and twists, but it doesn't break. Instead, it returns to its original shape once the pressure is released. That's what resilience does for you—it helps you recover from stress and challenges without losing your shape."

Ram leaned forward, intrigued. "So, resilience is about being flexible and bouncing back?"

"Exactly," Rishi said with a nod. "But it's more than just bouncing back—learning and growing from those experiences. Each time you stretch that rubber band, it becomes more pliable and stronger.

Similarly, every challenge you face and overcome makes you more resilient."

Rishi's tone became more instructive as he transitioned to practical advice. "So, how do you build and strengthen your resilience? Let me give you a few strategies that you can start practicing."

"First and foremost, embrace a Growth Mindset," Rishi began. "This is the belief that your abilities and intelligence can be developed through effort, learning, and persistence. When you face a setback, instead of seeing it as a failure, see it as an opportunity to learn and grow.

Ask yourself, 'What can I learn from this experience? How can it make me stronger?' This mindset is the foundation of resilience because it turns obstacles into steppingstones."

Priya smiled, recognizing the importance of this. "So, it's about seeing challenges as opportunities rather than threats."

"Exactly," Rishi confirmed. "With a growth mindset, every setback becomes a chance to improve. It's the difference between saying, 'I can't do this' and 'I can't do this yet.'"

"Next, strengthen your Locus of Control," Rishi continued. "This is the degree to which you believe you control the events in your life.

People with a strong internal locus of control believe that their actions influence their outcomes. They don't see themselves as victims of circumstance but as agents of change."

Ram looked thoughtful. "So, by focusing on what we can control, we become more resilient?"

"Precisely," Rishi said. "When you focus on what you can control, you take responsibility for your life. This empowers you to act, even in difficult situations.

Instead of being paralyzed by challenges, you ask yourself, 'What can I do about this?' And then you do it. This sense of control is crucial for resilience because it keeps you from feeling helpless."

Rishi's voice took on a more encouraging tone. "Another key aspect of resilience is Courage. This isn't just about-facing physical danger—it's about having the courage to keep going, to try again after failure, and to take risks in the face of uncertainty. Courage drives you to step out of your comfort zone and confront challenges head-on."

Priya nodded, inspired by the idea. "Courage allows us to take that first step, even when we're unsure of the outcome."

"Exactly," Rishi agreed. "And the more you practice courage, the more resilient you become. Every time you face a fear or take a risk, you build your resilience muscle. Remember, courage isn't the absence of fear—it's taking action despite it."

Rishi continued, "Another critical strategy is Emotional Regulation.

This ties back to Emotional Intelligence. Managing your emotions, especially during stressful situations, is crucial for resilience.

When faced with a challenge, it's normal to feel fear, anger, or frustration. But how you manage those emotions determines whether you'll be overwhelmed by the situation or rise above it."

Ram leaned in, curious. "How can we improve our emotional regulation?"

"One way," Rishi explained, "is through mindfulness practices like meditation or deep breathing.

These techniques help you stay calm and centered, even in stress. Another approach is cognitive reframing—changing the way you think about a situation. Instead of focusing on the negative aspects, try to find something positive or something you can learn from the experience."

Rishi's tone softened as he emphasized the final point. "Lastly, build Strong Relationships. Resilience isn't just about individual strength—it's also about having a support system.

Surround yourself with people who believe in you, who can offer encouragement and advice when you're facing tough times. Strong relationships provide the emotional support that helps you recover from setbacks more quickly."

Priya smiled, thinking of the people who had supported her during difficult times. "So, resilience isn't just about going it alone—it's also about knowing when to lean on others."

"Exactly," Rishi said. "Resilient people know that it's okay to ask for help and don't have to face challenges alone.

Whether it's friends, family, or colleagues, having a support network is crucial for bouncing back from adversity."

Rishi paused, letting the importance of these strategies sink in. "Connect resilience to what you've already learned CRITIC and Emotional Intelligence.

When you face a setback, use CRITIC to challenge assumptions about why things went wrong, research and evaluate new strategies, and plan how to approach the situation differently next time.

Your Emotional Intelligence will help you manage the emotional impact of setbacks, allowing you to stay calm and focused as you navigate through them."

Ram and Priya exchanged glances, seeing how everything they had learned was coming together.

Rishi leaned forward; his voice filled with quiet conviction. "Resilience isn't just about surviving challenges—it's about thriving despite them. It's about emerging from difficulties stronger, wiser, and more determined.

By cultivating a growth mindset, strengthening your locus of control, practicing courage, regulating your emotions, and building solid relationships, you'll be able to handle whatever comes your way and turn those challenges into opportunities for growth."

As the session concluded, they felt a deep sense of empowerment. Knowing how to build and practice resilience, they were ready to face whatever challenges lay ahead, knowing that each would make them stronger and more capable.

As Rishi wrapped up his discussion on resilience, he could see that Priya and Ram were beginning to grasp the importance of this critical skill.

6.7 Next Steps

It was the final evening of their intensive training, and the sun had just set over the hilltop cottage. A gentle breeze rustled the trees outside, carrying with it the soft sounds of nature. Inside, the warm glow of candles bathed the room in a cozy light. The table was set with a simple yet inviting meal, and Rishi gestured toward it with a welcoming smile.

"Come, let's take a break and enjoy a well-deserved dinner,"

Rishi said, his voice full of calm. "You've both worked incredibly hard these past days."

Priya and Ram sat down, grateful for the chance to pause. Yet, as the evening unfolded, there was a sense that Rishi had more to say.

The conversation began light and relaxed, but as dinner progressed, Rishi leaned back in his chair, his expression growing thoughtful.

"You know," Rishi began, looking at them with quiet intensity, "what you've learned here is significant."

Rishi chuckled softly. "You're both more than ready. You've already come so far. Trust what you've learned, and you'll build on it when the time is right. For now, focus on the upcoming presentation. Everything you need to succeed tomorrow is already within you."

Priya and Ram exchanged glances, feeling a renewed sense of confidence. The vastness of what lay ahead no longer seemed daunting—it felt like the beginning of an exciting journey, one they were now eager to embark on.

Rishi raised his glass, a warm smile spreading across his face. "To growth, to learning, and success. This is just the beginning."

Priya and Ram lifted their glasses, their doubts replaced by quiet determination and anticipation for the future.

The air was filled with a sense of quiet accomplishment as Priya and Ram sat across from Rishi, their notebooks full and their minds buzzing with new insights. They had spent the past days learning, reflecting, and growing, and now, the time had come to put all they had learned into practice.

Rishi looked at them both with a satisfied smile. "You've come a long way in a short time. You've learned about Emotional Intelligence, Critical Thinking, Resilience, and more. But remember, knowledge alone isn't enough—how you apply it truly matters."

Priya nodded, feeling the weight of his words. "We're ready, Rishi. We want to use everything we've learned to its fullest potential."

Ram added, his voice filled with determination, "We know this is just the beginning. We're excited to put these skills into practice, but we want to ensure we're doing it right."

Rishi leaned forward, his expression severe but encouraging. "Here's what I want you to do. First, make these skills a part of your daily routine. Don't wait for a crisis or a big project to practice them—start using them in small ways every day.

For example, practice Emotional Intelligence by being more mindful of your emotions and those of others in every interaction.

Use Critical Thinking to evaluate the information you encounter, whether in meetings, reading reports, or making decisions."

Priya took a deep breath, feeling the clarity of his advice. "So, it's about integrating these skills into everything we do, not just when we face big challenges."

"Exactly," Rishi confirmed. "And when it comes to Resilience, remember the analogies we discussed—the rubber band and the bamboo tree.

When you face setbacks, don't just bounce back—use those experiences to grow stronger. Embrace a growth mindset, focus on what you can control, and don't fear taking risks. Courage and resilience go hand in hand."

Ram smiled, feeling a surge of confidence. "We are determined to transform our challenges into opportunities."

Rishi nodded, pleased with their resolve. "That's the spirit. And one more thing—don't forget the importance of reflection.

After every significant decision, project, or even a difficult conversation, take the time to reflect.

What did you do well? What could you improve next time?

This ongoing reflection will help refine your skills and become even more effective."

Priya and Ram exchanged glances, both feeling a deep sense of empowerment.

They knew they had the tools they needed to succeed, and more importantly, they knew how to apply them.

Priya spoke first, her voice filled with gratitude. "Rishi, we can't thank you enough.

What you've taught us—these are lessons we'll carry with us for the rest of our lives. We feel ready, not just for this project, but for anything that comes our way."

Ram nodded in agreement; his eyes bright with excitement. "You've given us more than just knowledge—you've given us the confidence to face whatever challenges lie ahead. We're grateful for everything."

Rishi's smile widened, his tone warm and encouraging. "You've both worked hard, and you've earned this confidence. Now, go out there and apply what you've learned. Remember, this is just the beginning of your journey.

Continue to learn, grow, and push yourselves. And most importantly, stay true to the principles you've learned here—they'll guide you well."

With that, Rishi stood up, extending a hand to each of them. "Good luck. I have no doubt you'll both go far."

Priya and Ram shook his hand, their hearts full of gratitude and excitement. As they left the cottage, stepping out into the fresh evening air, they felt a renewed sense of purpose.

The path ahead was still challenging, but they were ready for it—armed with new knowledge, a stronger mindset, and the resilience to turn any obstacle into an opportunity.

Walking down the hill together, they couldn't help but smile. The journey with Rishi had been transformative, and now they were eager to start the next chapter of their careers, confident that they had what it took to succeed—not just in their current project but in every aspect of their lives.

Section 3

Application and Victory

Chapter 7

The pre-final frontier

Practical Application, Unforeseen Challenges

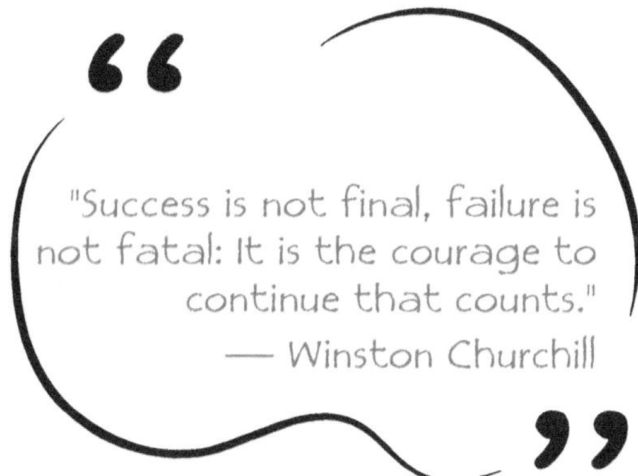

With the frameworks fresh in their minds, Priya and Ram returned to their desks at ClickFlix, determined to put everything they had learned into practice. The next week was critical; it was their last chance to perfect their report and presentation before the final client meeting.

As they began working, the pressure was palpable. Every decision felt like it carried the weight of their careers. They knew that this wasn't just about following the frameworks—they had to think critically, be creative, and anticipate any challenges that might arise.

Their initial confidence was soon tested when an unexpected email from Atul arrived. The client, who had previously seemed satisfied with their direction, now had a series of new, last-minute requirements and concerns. The changes were substantial enough to force Priya and Ram to rethink their entire approach.

'This is a major setback,' Ram said, frustration evident in his voice. 'We're going to have to redo a lot of the work we've already completed.'

Priya took a deep breath, trying to stay calm. 'We can't afford to lose our cool now. Let's break this down using the SSOLVER framework and tackle these issues one by one.'

They spent the next several hours working through the SSOLVER framework, setting the stage by realigning their goals with the new requirements.

They separated the emotional response from the actual problem, focusing on what needed to be done rather than the stress they were feeling.

'We need to overcome our biases and look at this from the client's perspective,' Priya said. 'Atul isn't trying to make our lives difficult—he just wants the best possible outcome. Let's approach this with a learner mindset and figure out how we can exceed his expectations.'
As if the client's demands weren't enough, Priya and Ram soon found themselves dealing with internal conflicts within their team.

Different departments were at odds over resource allocation, with some members feeling overburdened while others were left out of the loop. The tension threatened to derail their progress just as they were getting back on track.

'This is the last thing we need right now,' Ram muttered, rubbing his temples. 'We're running out of time, and now we have to play peacemakers.'

'We can't ignore this,' Priya said firmly. 'Let's use the COALESCE framework to bring everyone back together. We need to connect, organize, and align our team so that we're all moving in the same direction.'

As they worked to resolve the team issues, another problem surfaced—key resources that were critical to completing the project on time suddenly became unavailable.

Equipment failures, scheduling conflicts, and personal emergencies within the team all conspired to push them further behind schedule.

'Can anything else go wrong?' Ram exclaimed, exasperation creeping into his voice. 'At this rate, we're not going to make the deadline.'

'We have to stay focused,' Priya replied, though she was feeling the strain as well.

'We need to prioritize what truly matters and make the best use of what we have. Let's use the PRIORITIZE framework to reassess our tasks and eliminate any non-essential activities.'

Despite the setbacks, Priya and Ram pushed forward with renewed determination. They worked late into the night, every night, making sacrifices and doing whatever it took to stay on track. But the pressure was immense, and the toll it was taking on them was becoming increasingly evident.

'We're almost there,' Priya said one night, her voice tinged with exhaustion. 'But we can't afford any more mistakes. We need to double-check everything and make sure we're prepared for any questions or challenges that might come our way.'

'Agreed,' Ram replied, equally tired but resolute. 'We've come too far to let anything slip through the cracks now.

Let's go through the CLEAR framework for our written communication and the PEACE framework for how we'll handle the presentation.'

With just 24 hours left before the final client meeting, Priya and Ram reviewed their work one last time. They knew they had done everything they could, but the uncertainty lingered.

Would it be enough? They had faced so many obstacles, and the thought of one more unforeseen challenge was almost too much to bear.

'No matter what happens tomorrow,' Priya said, trying to bolster their spirits, 'we've given it our all.

We've dealt with every challenge, and we're as prepared as we can be.'

'Let's just hope that's enough,' Ram added quietly. The weight of their journey was evident in his voice, but so was his quiet determination.

As they finally left the office the night before D-Day, they couldn't shake the feeling that the toughest test was yet to come.

Chapter 8 — **D-day and triumph**

Victory Through Preparedness

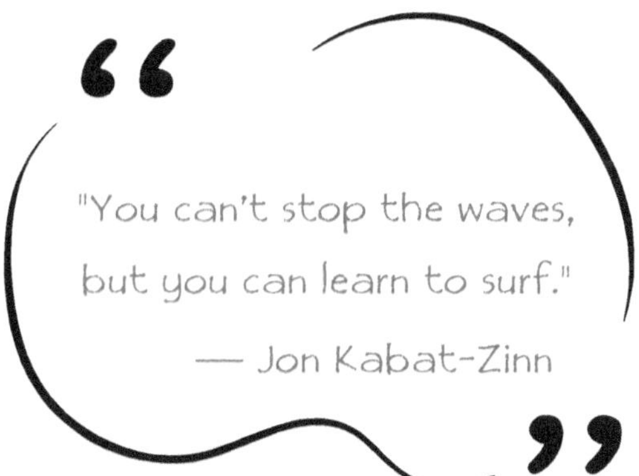

The morning of the client meeting arrived with a mix of nerves and excitement, but beneath that surface tension, a sense of foreboding lingered. Priya and Ram had barely slept, their minds racing with everything they had prepared for.

Today was the day they would face Atul and present the culmination of weeks of hard work, learning, and growth. But as they arrived at the office, they couldn't shake the feeling that something was about to go wrong.
As they entered the boardroom, the atmosphere was electric, charged with both anticipation and anxiety.

Colleagues wished them luck, sensing the importance of the moment. Sharma, the CEO, was already seated, his expression one of quiet confidence, though Priya noticed a tightness around his eyes that hadn't been there before.

He had seen the transformation in Priya and Ram, but even he knew that the stakes today were higher than they had ever been.

Atul arrived, greeted everyone with a firm handshake, and settled into his seat. The room fell silent as Priya and Ram stood at the front, ready to begin.

But just as Priya was about to speak, the door to the boardroom swung open unexpectedly. A middle-aged man in a crisp suit walked in, followed by two other stern-looking individuals.

The tension in the room spiked immediately.

'Who are they?' Ram whispered, leaning toward Priya, his voice barely audible.

'I don't know,' Priya replied, her heart pounding. 'But this wasn't part of the plan.'

Atul cleared his throat, breaking the uneasy silence. 'I apologize for the surprise,' he said, addressing the room.

'These are senior executives from our headquarters. Given the size of this project, they wanted to be part of the decision-making process. I hope you don't mind.'
Priya and Ram exchanged a quick, tense glance.

This was a curveball they hadn't anticipated.

Presenting to Atul was one thing, but now they had to impress a whole new set of decision-makers, who hadn't been part of the process up until now. The stakes had just been raised, and they had no idea what these new players would expect or how they would respond.

'Of course, we're happy to have you here,' Priya managed to say, forcing a smile. 'Let's get started, then.' But inside, her mind was racing.

They would have to adapt their presentation on the fly, considering this new audience and the implications it brought.

They moved into their presentation, but the usual flow they had rehearsed felt off. The new executives interrupted frequently, asking pointed questions that were more aggressive than what they had prepared for.

Ram struggled to keep up, his confidence wavering with each unexpected query.

'What about the long-term sustainability of this strategy?' one of the executives asked, his tone skeptical. 'Have you considered the potential risks to our core business?'

Ram hesitated, searching for the right words. 'We've accounted for those factors,' he began, but the executive cut him off before he could finish.

'I'm not convinced,' the executive said bluntly. 'This feels like a short-term fix rather than a sustainable solution.'

Priya felt the blood drain from her face. They were losing control of the narrative, and the confidence they had built was slipping away. She knew they had to regain the upper hand, but how?

Just as Priya was about to respond, the unthinkable happened. The screen behind them, which had been displaying their carefully crafted slides, suddenly went black. The projector flickered, and a loud, jarring noise filled the room as the entire system crashed.

'What's happening?' Sharma demanded, his voice tight with tension.

Ram scrambled to the laptop, frantically trying to reboot the system, but nothing was working. Priya could see the expressions of the executives hardening—this was the worst possible time for a technical failure.

'We're experiencing a technical difficulty,' Priya said, trying to keep her voice calm despite the panic rising inside her. 'Give us a moment to sort this out.' But she knew they didn't have a moment. They needed to act fast, or they risked losing everything.

Realizing that they couldn't afford to wait, Priya made a split-second decision. 'Ram, forget the slides,' she said firmly. 'We'll continue without them.'

Ram looked at her in shock. 'Are you sure?'
'We don't have a choice,' Priya replied, turning back to the room. 'Let's proceed with the discussion. We can address any concerns directly.'

With no visuals to rely on, Priya and Ram had to pivot entirely to a discussion format, addressing the executives' concerns head-on. They applied the PEACE framework, maintaining composure under pressure, and used the COALESCE framework to bring the conversation back to their key points.

'We understand your concerns about sustainability,' Priya said, her voice steady and confident. 'Our strategy is built on flexibility and resilience, designed to adapt as market conditions change. Let's explore how we've accounted for potential risks in the long term.'

The room was silent as they continued, but slowly, the atmosphere began to shift. The executives started to engage more positively, and Atul watched with renewed interest.

Priya and Ram had managed to turn a disastrous situation into an opportunity to demonstrate their deep understanding and adaptability.

Just as they were beginning to regain their footing, the door opened again, and yet another figure walked in.

This time, it was Rishi. Priya and Ram's mentor entered the room without a word, took a seat at the back, and observed.

His presence added a new layer of tension—they hadn't expected him to show up.

Sharma's eyebrows shot up in surprise, but he didn't say anything. Priya felt her heart skip a beat—why was Rishi here? Was he there to support them, or was this another test?

'Please continue,' Rishi said calmly, his voice carrying an unspoken challenge. It was as if he was daring them to prove that they had truly internalized everything he had taught them.

With Rishi's eyes on them, Priya and Ram pushed forward with renewed determination. They delved deeper into their analysis, responded to every question with clarity and insight, and didn't shy away from difficult topics. They used every framework at their disposal, turning the challenging situation into a showcase of their skills.

Finally, after what felt like an eternity, Atul leaned back in his chair and exchanged a look with the executives. The room was thick with anticipation.

'This is impressive,' Atul finally said, breaking the silence. 'You've managed to turn a challenging situation into a demonstration of your capability.

Despite the obstacles, you've shown that you're adaptable, knowledgeable, and committed to delivering value. I'm convinced—let's move forward with this project.'

The relief was palpable as Priya and Ram finally allowed themselves to breathe. They had done it—they had won the contract against all odds.

The room erupted in applause, and even Rishi nodded in approval from the back of the room.

'Well done,' Sharma said, shaking their hands with genuine pride. 'You've exceeded all expectations.'

As the meeting wrapped up, Priya and Ram took a moment to absorb the significance of what they had achieved.

They had faced their fears, overcome unexpected challenges, and emerged victorious. The journey had tested their limits, but it had also revealed their true potential.

That evening, the team celebrated their success, but there was also a sense of anticipation in the air.

Sharma pulled Priya and Ram aside, his expression serious yet excited. 'I received a call from another large client today,' he said. 'They're interested in a project that's ten times the size of this one. I want you two to lead it.'

Priya and Ram exchanged a look of excitement and determination.

They knew the journey ahead would be even more challenging, but they were ready. They had been forged in fire, and they were ready to face whatever came next.

<table>
<tr><td>Chapter
9</td><td># The next challenge</td></tr>
</table>

A Journey of Infinite Possibilities

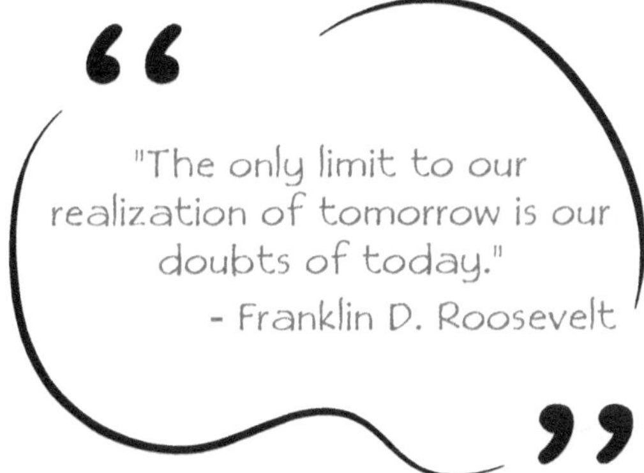

The celebration had wound down, and the office was quiet again. Priya and Ram stood by the large windows overlooking the city, reflecting on the journey that had brought them here. The glow of their recent success still warmed them, but their minds were already racing ahead to the future.

'It's hard to believe how much has changed in such a short time,' Priya mused, watching the city lights flicker below. 'We've gone from barely holding on to leading some of the biggest projects in the company.'

'And we're just getting started,' Ram added with a grin. 'Sharma's new project is going to be a challenge, but after everything we've been through, I feel like we can handle anything.'

They both knew that the journey they had undertaken wasn't just about mastering frameworks or winning a contract. It was about discovering their own potential, building resilience, and learning to lead with confidence and empathy.

The lessons they had learned from Rishi and the challenges they had faced together had transformed them in ways they were only beginning to understand.

'Rishi was right about one thing,' Priya said thoughtfully. 'AI and tools are just enablers. It's our ability to think critically, connect with people, and tell compelling stories that makes the real difference. That's what clients like Atul are looking for—partners who can see beyond the data and understand the bigger picture.'

'And it's not just about clients,' Ram added. 'It's about how we lead our teams, how we handle challenges, and how we keep growing, both professionally and personally.

The frameworks are great, but it's the mindset shift that has been the most important part of this journey.'

As they talked, Sharma joined them by the window. 'I've been watching you both closely,' he said, his tone serious but filled with pride. 'You've proven yourselves in ways that go far beyond just winning a contract. You've shown that you're ready to take on bigger challenges, to lead with purpose and vision.'

'The new project is going to be a significant step up,' Sharma continued. 'It's going to test everything you've learned and push you even further. But I have no doubt that you're ready for it.'

Priya and Ram exchanged a look, a mix of excitement and determination in their eyes.

They knew that the road ahead would be difficult, but they were no longer afraid of the challenges.

They had been forged in fire, and they were ready to face whatever came next.

As they left the office that night, the future felt wide open, filled with infinite possibilities. They had learned that success wasn't just about achieving a goal, but about the journey itself—the growth, the learning, and the resilience that came from facing challenges head-on.

Priya looked up at the night sky, feeling a deep sense of gratitude. 'This is just the beginning,' she said softly.

'It is,' Ram agreed, his voice filled with quiet confidence. 'And I can't wait to see where the journey takes us next.'

With that, they walked into the night, ready to embrace the next chapter of their journey, knowing that no matter what challenges lay ahead, they had the skills, the mindset, and the resilience to overcome them.

The future was bright, and they were ready to make the most of it.

Section 4

Beyond the Journey.
Reflect, Apply, and Grow

Chapter 10

Reflection

"We do not learn from experience... we learn from reflecting on experience." — John Dewey

The story of Priya and Ram is not just one of overcoming challenges—it's a story of transformation, of growth, and of the endless possibilities that lie ahead for those who are willing to learn, adapt, and persevere. As you turn the final page of this book, remember that your own journey is filled with infinite possibilities.

The frameworks, skills, and lessons you've learned are tools to help you navigate your path, but the journey itself is yours to define.

Whether you're facing a daunting challenge, striving for a breakthrough, or simply seeking to grow, remember that every step you take is a step toward becoming the person you are meant to be. Embrace the journey with courage, curiosity, and resilience, and know that the possibilities are truly infinite.

As you move forward, let this story serve as a reminder that the real journey never ends—it only evolves, with each new challenge bringing you closer to your true potential.

1. Reflection: The Power of Looking Back

As Priya and Ram have experienced throughout their journey, reflection is a critical component of growth and development. Now, it's your turn to engage in this process. Reflection allows you to solidify your understanding, draw connections between different concepts, and identify areas where you can continue to improve.

Why is Reflection Important?

Internalizing Knowledge: Reflection helps you move from simply understanding a concept to genuinely internalizing it. When you take the time to reflect, you transform theoretical knowledge into practical wisdom.

Identifying Patterns: Reflecting on your experiences can help you identify patterns in your behavior, decision-making, and emotional responses. This awareness is the first step toward making meaningful changes.

Learning from Experience: Reflection allows you to learn from successes and failures. When you analyze what went well and what didn't, you gain insights that can guide your actions.

Enhancing Emotional Intelligence: Reflection helps you develop greater self-awareness and empathy by encouraging you to consider your own emotions and the emotions of others involved in your experiences.

2. Guided Reflection Exercises

To help you get started with your reflection, here are some guided exercises:

Exercise 1: Reflect on Emotional Intelligence

Think about a recent interaction where your emotions influenced your behavior. How did you manage those emotions? What could you have done differently to achieve a better outcome?

Consider a situation where you noticed someone else's emotions affecting their behavior. How did you respond? What did you learn from that experience about empathy and social awareness?

Exercise 2: Reflect on Critical Thinking

Identify a recent decision you made. What assumptions did you make during the decision-making process? Were those assumptions valid? How did they impact the outcome?
Think about a situation where you needed to gather and evaluate information before making a decision. How thorough were you in your research? Did you consider alternative perspectives? What would you do differently next time?

Exercise 3: Reflect on Resilience

Recall a time when you faced a significant challenge or setback. How did you respond? Did you demonstrate resilience? What did you learn from that experience about your ability to bounce back and grow?

Think about a situation where you had to manage stress or adversity. What strategies did you use to stay calm and focused? How can you strengthen your resilience for future challenges?

3. Personal Reflection Journal

Consider keeping a personal reflection journal where you regularly document your thoughts, experiences, and insights. Use the following prompts to guide your journaling practice:

- What have I learned today? How can I apply this lesson in my life?
- What challenges did I face today, and how did I respond? What could I have done differently?
- How did I manage my emotions in difficult situations? How did others' emotions affect me?
- What decisions did I make today? How did I apply critical thinking to those decisions?
- How did I demonstrate resilience today? What helped me stay strong, and what can I improve?

4. Reflection on Your Growth Journey

As you reflect, take some time to think about how you've grown throughout your journey. Consider the following:

Your Personal Growth: How have you changed since you began this journey? What new skills or perspectives have you developed?

Your Professional Growth: How has your approach to your work or leadership evolved? What new strategies or frameworks have you implemented?

Your Emotional Growth: How has your emotional intelligence improved? How has this impacted your relationships, both professionally and personally?

Your Resilience: How have you become more resilient? What challenges have you overcome, and how have they made you stronger?

Closing thoughts: Beyond AI

The True Drivers of Success

As Priya and Ram reflect on their journey, it becomes clear that their transformation wasn't just about mastering AI tools or achieving quick wins.

While technology and productivity tools play a role in modern work, the real breakthroughs came from something more profound—something more fundamentally human.

In today's fast-paced, technology-driven world, it is easy to get caught up in the allure of AI, automation, and perceived productivity gains.

But true success, Priya and Ram discovered, isn't about relying solely on tools and shortcuts. It's about applying deep thought, understanding each stakeholder's "What's In It For Me?" (WIIFM), and using that insight to drive meaningful action.

Throughout their journey, Priya and Ram learned the value of Emotional Intelligence—understanding their emotions and those of others, managing relationships with empathy, and gracefully navigating complex interpersonal dynamics.

They realized that no matter how advanced the technology, it's the human element—connecting with others personally— that truly drives success.

Critical Thinking played a crucial role as well. It's not enough to follow trends or jump to conclusions in a world awash with information. Priya and Ram learned to challenge assumptions, gather and analyze data, and consider the broader implications of their decisions.

This deliberate approach enabled them to make informed, strategic choices that aligned with their goals and their stakeholders' needs.

Confidence and Resilience were their steadfast companions through the ups and downs. They faced setbacks, doubts, and failures but didn't let those define them.

Instead, they used every challenge as an opportunity to learn, grow, and return stronger. Their resilience allowed them to stay the course, even when the path was difficult, and their confidence gave them the courage to take bold steps when it mattered most.

Ultimately, it wasn't AI or any other tool that defined their success. They could combine these human skills—emotional Intelligence, Critical Thinking, Confidence, and Resilience—with a relentless pursuit of excellence and a deep understanding of their stakeholders' needs.

As you close this book and return to your professional challenges, remember that while technology can enhance your productivity, these core human skills will truly set you apart.

In every decision, every interaction, and every challenge you face, ask yourself:

- Am I applying deep thought?
- Am I considering the perspectives and needs of others?
- Am I using my Emotional Intelligence?
- Am I thinking critically about the situation?
- Am I staying resilient in the face of adversity?

Success in today's workplace isn't about finding the quickest solution—it's about finding the right one.

It's about leading with empathy, thinking strategically, and having the grit to see things through.

As Priya and Ram have shown, these qualities will not only help you succeed but also allow you to thrive in an ever-changing world.

Your journey is just beginning, and the possibilities are endless. Embrace these lessons, apply them with intention, and watch as you navigate your career with newfound confidence and clarity.

Chapter 11

Practical application

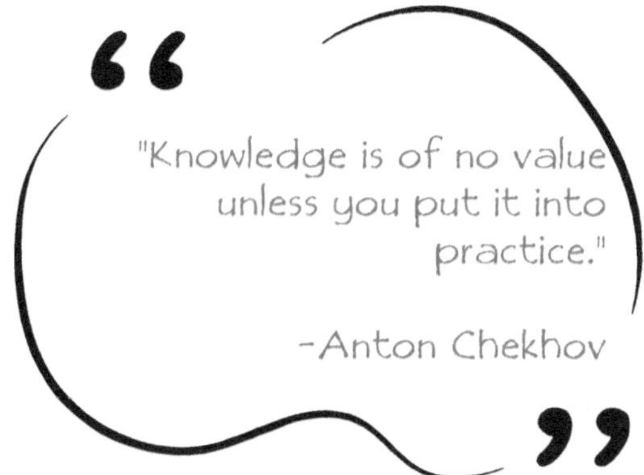

Mind map – SuRaM's business frameworks

#	To achieve this objective…	Use this framework…
1	Are you establishing or reinforcing your leadership credibility?	ACCREDIIT
2	Are you trying to engage, inspire, or persuade your team or stakeholders?	GREAT VIBES
3	Do you want to improve clarity in your communication and conversation?	CLEAR PATH
4	Are you crafting a presentation or a narrative that needs to resonate with your audience?	PRESENT
5	Do you want to engage the listeners while narrating a business topic?	STORY
6	Are you dealing with a conflict within your team or between departments?	CONCUR
7	Are you facing a complex problem that requires a thorough analysis and a methodical solution?	SOLVER
8	Are you supporting a team member through personal or professional challenges?	HEALER
9	Are you analysing data to inform a decision or identify trends?	INSIGHT
10	Are you leading your team through a period of significant change?	CHANGE

#	To achieve this objective…	Use this framework…
11	Are you prioritizing tasks or managing multiple competing demands?	PRIORITIZE
12	Are you facilitating collaboration across teams or departments?	COALESCE

ACCREDIIT: Building Authenticity and Trust

Pause and take a moment to reflect:

- Do your team members, colleagues, or clients need to recognize you as a competent leader?
- Do you struggle to earn the trust of your peers, no matter how hard you try?
- Are you perceived as inauthentic or need to be clearer in your decision-making?
- Do your leadership efforts seem to be noticed or appreciated?
- Are people around you not taking your ideas seriously, even though you know they're valuable?

Develop credibility and authenticity with the ACCREDIIT framework. Learn how to earn trust, build genuine relationships, and make sure your leadership presence is felt across the board.

GREAT VIBEs: Enhancing Team Engagement and Motivation

- Do you need help with team members who seem disengaged and uninterested in their work?

- Do your requests for collaboration often go ignored or half-heartedly followed?

- Do you look for help to inspire your team to go above and beyond?

- Do your team meetings feel like they drain energy instead of motivating action?

- Are your efforts to build team culture falling flat, with no visible change in morale?

With the GREAT VIBE framework, understand the power of engagement. Learn how to create an atmosphere where your team is motivated, energized, and fully aligned with your vision.

CLEAR PATH: Communicating Your Ideas Clearly and Effectively

- Do you need help explaining your viewpoints clearly, especially in complex situations?
- Do your ideas often need to be more explicit in translation, leaving others confused or frustrated?
- Are you having trouble keeping people engaged during meaningful discussions or presentations?
- Do you find it hard to respond thoughtfully in high-pressure moments?
- Do your messages frequently need to be understood or understood by your team?

Discover the art of clear communication with the CLEAR PATH framework. Learn how to focus, listen, analyze, and articulate your ideas precisely so that your messages resonate.

PRESENT: Mastering Presentation and Public Speaking

- Do you get nervous or need help with your words when giving presentations?
- Do your presentations need more impact, leaving your audience bored or disengaged?
- Do you struggle to structure your ideas clearly and compellingly?
- Are you unsure how to capture your audience's attention and keep them engaged throughout?
- Do you need help handling tough questions or interruptions during your presentations?

Learn how to present with confidence using the PRESENT framework. You'll discover how to structure your ideas, engage your audience, and deliver powerful presentations that leave a lasting impression.

STORY: Using Storytelling to Influence and Inspire

- Do your presentations and communications feel dry or dull?
- Are you struggling to make an emotional connection with your audience?
- Do people seem to forget your message soon after you've delivered it?
- Do you need help getting buy-in for your ideas or proposals?
- Do you wish you could inspire and influence your audience but don't know how?

Explore the power of storytelling with the STORY framework. Learn how to turn dry data into compelling narratives that inspire action and influence your audience more deeply.

SSOLVER: Structured Problem-Solving for Leadership Success

- Do you feel overwhelmed by the constant stream of problems coming your way?
- Do personal conflicts within the team derail your problem-solving efforts?
- Do you find it difficult to focus on the problem because of biases and misunderstandings?
- Is your team struggling to develop creative solutions when faced with challenges?
- Are your attempts to solve issues often met with resistance and poor execution?

Use the SSOLVER framework to approach problem-solving in a structured, effective way. You'll learn how to separate emotions from the issue, foster creativity, and lead your team to solutions that work.

CONCUR: Handling Conflicts and Finding Common Ground

- Are you constantly facing conflicts within your team and unable to resolve them?
- Do you find it hard to get opposing sides to agree on common goals?
- Are your efforts to mediate conflicts often met with resistance or frustration?
- Do disagreements between team members hold up progress on important projects?
- Is your team divided, with no clear path to reconciliation?

The CONCUR framework will help you resolve conflicts by focusing on commitment, common ground, and building unity. Learn how to manage difficult situations and bring harmony back to your team.

HEALER: Leading with Empathy and Emotional Intelligence

- Do you have team members who are struggling, but you don't know how to support them?
- Are your attempts to empathize with others often misunderstood or seen as a weakness?
- Do you worry that your team doesn't feel heard or understood by you as their leader?
- Is it hard to balance empathy with the need for results and productivity?
- Are team members becoming disengaged because they feel disconnected from leadership?

Learn how to lead with empathy using the HEALER framework. This method will help you connect with your team emotionally, support them through challenges, and keep them motivated without sacrificing results.

CHANGE: Managing Change and Uncertainty

- Are you finding it hard to lead your team through change and uncertainty?
- Do your team members resist new ideas or processes, making change difficult?
- Do you need help communicating the reasons for change in a way your team understands and accepts?
- Is it challenging to keep your team motivated and productive during times of transition?
- Are you unsure how to manage your own stress and anxiety while leading through change?

Master the art of change management with the CHANGE framework. Learn how to lead your team through uncertainty, communicate the benefits of change, and confidently handle resistance.

PRIORITIZE: Staying Focused and Managing Time Effectively

- Do you feel overwhelmed by the sheer number of tasks and responsibilities on your plate?
- Are you constantly firefighting, dealing with urgent issues rather than focusing on what truly matters?
- Do you struggle to prioritize your tasks and feel like you're not making real progress?
- Do you need help managing your time effectively while remaining available to your team?
- Is it difficult for you to say no to less critical tasks or requests, even when they derail your focus?

Learn how to prioritize your tasks and focus on what matters most with the PRIORITIZE framework. You'll discover how to manage your time, reduce stress, and stay focused on the goals that will make the most significant impact.

NEGOTIATE: Mastering the Art of Negotiation

- Do you often walk away from negotiations feeling like you've compromised too much?
- Are you unsure of how to prepare for tough negotiations, especially when the stakes are high?
- Do you struggle to find common ground in difficult negotiations, leaving both parties unsatisfied?
- Are you worried that your negotiation tactics are seen as too aggressive or too passive?
- Is it difficult for you to adapt your approach when negotiations don't go as planned?

The NEGOTIATE framework will give you a step-by-step approach to negotiate with confidence and strength. Learn how to find win-win solutions and walk away from the table with outcomes you're proud of.

MEDIATE: Resolving Conflicts Without Taking Sides

- Do you feel stuck between two sides of a conflict with no idea how to mediate effectively?
- Are you worried that your involvement in team conflicts will be seen as biased?
- Do attempts to resolve conflicts often backfire or leave both parties feeling unsatisfied?
- Is your team's productivity suffering because of ongoing disputes that you can't seem to resolve?
- Do you struggle to find solutions that satisfy both parties in a conflict?

Use the MEDIATE framework to resolve conflict with neutrality, empathy, and fairness. You'll learn how to facilitate discussions, identify solutions, and ensure both parties feel heard and respected.

CRUCIAL: Navigating High-Stakes Conversations with Confidence

- Are you avoiding difficult conversations because you're afraid of the fallout?
- Do high-stakes discussions often leave you feeling drained or anxious?
- Are your attempts to address sensitive issues seen as confrontational or unhelpful?
- Do you find it difficult to balance emotions with logic during tough conversations?
- Are your high-pressure discussions leading to misunderstandings or unresolved tensions?

The CRUCIAL framework will help you navigate tough conversations with clarity, empathy, and confidence. Learn how to manage high-pressure talks without losing control or causing unnecessary tension.

DELICATE: Managing Sensitive Issues with Care

- Do you feel like you're walking on eggshells when dealing with sensitive topics?
- Are your efforts to handle delicate situations sometimes making things worse instead of better?
- Do you struggle to find the right words when addressing emotional or personal issues within your team?
- Are you worried about hurting feelings or causing offense when dealing with sensitive topics?
- Is it hard for you to maintain clarity and professionalism in emotionally charged conversations?

The DELICATE framework will help you approach sensitive situations with empathy, clarity, and care. Learn how to manage delicate issues without causing harm, ensuring that both emotions and facts are respected.

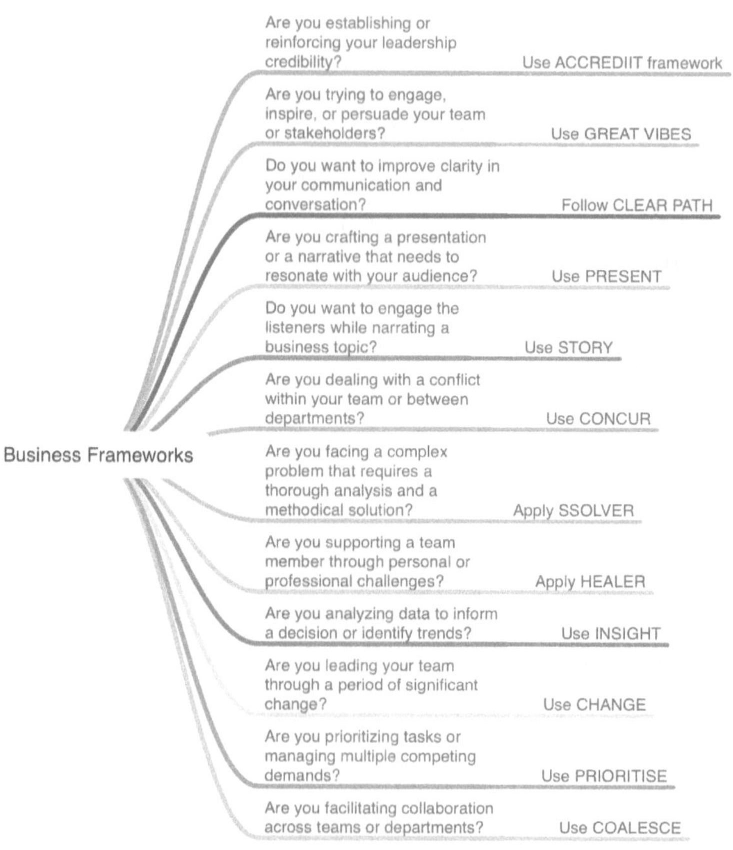

Visit https://www.futureproofleader.in/fitf to use the online version.

About the author

SuRaM is a business transformation leader with strong people, process, and technology alignment expertise.

He founded SkillCulture™, a digital ecosystem for career seekers, coaches, and corporates.

SuRaM architected and implemented 12 enterprise platforms during the last two decades.

SuRaM has authored six books and created over 50 e-learning courses on career success, personality development, professional development, and various other leadership genres.

He is also a Certified Professional Scrum Master I, AWS Certified Cloud Practitioner, Certified Professional in OKR™, and a registered Independent Director.

Before setting up SkillCulture, he worked as Executive Director- Karvy Insurance Repository and as CTO – Karvy Fintech.

He has over 30 years of experience in technology across BFSI domains. During this tenure, Suram has established various business lines, enterprise IT applications, and digital platforms.

Awards

- Best book award – Gold – "Growth Quotient"
- Best book award – Sliver– "Slide Spin"
- CIO Next Award
- CEO Insights – Top 10 leaders in Hyderabad Start-ups -2022

Also from SuRaM

The following books are available both in Kindle and Print Formats:

- Office Epidemics
- Growth Quotients
- Digi Guru
- Career Compass

- Slide Spin - Presentation Sense
- Slide Spin - Personal Workbook

SuRaM has also authored over 40 e-learning courses on Leadership, Technology, and Management Genres.

Please visit https://clap.skillculture.in for more details.

Go to his Author Page on Amazon

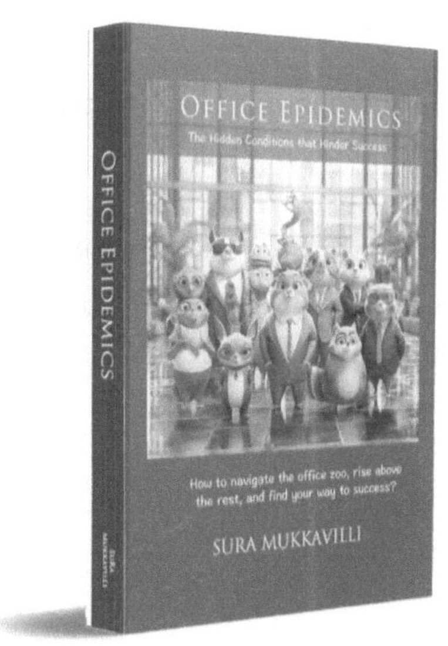

OFFICE EPIDEMICS

Behind every missed deadline, awkward meeting, or frustrating project lies an untold story of workplace chaos...

What if the root cause of your team's struggles isn't lack of skills or resources, but something deeper—an office epidemic?

In Office Epidemics: The Hidden Conditions That Hinder Success, we take a unique approach, introducing you to the often-overlooked creatures who lurk in every modern workplace, wreaking havoc on productivity and career growth.

- **Micromanagitis:** The Ant who never lets go of control.

- **Pissilepsy:** The raging Bull that charges at the most minor issues.
- **Procrastinitis:** The lounging Cat who delays and derails everything.

Whether you're a seasoned leader or just trying to survive office politics, this book is for you.

It will open your eyes to the real reasons behind everyday frustrations and help you diagnose the hidden conditions affecting your team and yourself. It's time to regain control of your career.

Are you ready to discover who's really holding you back?
Find out now before it's too late.